Leadership Management Toolbox

A set of tools to assist you in the art of leading and managing your most valued assets—your employees

If you're not aware of and using these tools, you're wasting time and money.

These processes will show you how to translate strategic vision (your view of the future) into day-to-day action items.

In so doing, you will be able to focus, align, communicate, and track resource allocation, and take your organization to the next level in the midst of diminishing resources

LEADERSHIP MANAGEMENT TOOLBOX

A COLLECTION OF THE BEST TOOLS, TECHNIQUES AND PROCEDURES TO MANAGE AND LEAD YOUR EMPLOYEES

PAT THOMAS

Copyright © 2011 by Pat Thomas.

Library of Congress Control Number: 2011905183
ISBN: Hardcover 978-1-4568-9862-5
Softcover 978-1-4568-9861-8
Ebook 978-1-4568-9863-2

All rights reserved. No part of this book may be reproduced or transmitted in any form or by any means, electronic or mechanical, including photocopying, recording, or by any information storage and retrieval system, without permission in writing from the copyright owner.

This book was printed in the United States of America.

To order additional copies of this book, contact:
Xlibris Corporation
1-888-795-4274
www.Xlibris.com
Orders@Xlibris.com
96028

CONTENTS

Chapter One	Communication	
	(Our Most Important yet Least Understood) Process............	21
Chapter Two	Defining and Guiding Leadership	45
Chapter Three	Change Management...	61
Chapter Four	How to Conduct an Effective Meeting	
	(Working Group Management)..	71
Chapter Five	Parlor Tricks..	76
Chapter Six	Balanced Scorecard, Lean/Sixth Sigma, and	
	Other Process Improvement Activities	79
Chapter Seven	How to Conduct an Adequate After-Action Review	114
Chapter Eight	How to Develop and Implement Corrective Action Plan Your	
	Customer Will Accept..	119

Summary Conclusion... 127
Acknowledgments... 131
Pat Thomas Resume 133
Program Management Experience... 133
End Notes: Sources of Information 137
Index.. 139

WHY LEADERSHIP MANAGEMENT?

Introduction

Today's business environment continues to change over time. It appears that the margins seem to be getting smaller each year while success continues to be redefined and is harder to accomplish. The question becomes, "How do we get from here to there in today's industrial environment with today's economy?" We know what we want to accomplish and have smart, good people working for us, but we just can't seem to make the connection between strategic planning and successful execution. Where's the magic in our organizational processes and procedures that will allow us to be successful? How do we use the people and tools provided to show a profit and meet the expectations of our customers year after year? When it comes to efficiency, our shareholder's management expectation is for us to become twice as effective for half of what it costs to perform the same tasks last year. A corollary to Moore's law no. 1 (which states that the number of transistors on a chip doubles every twenty-four months coined by Intel cofounder, Gordon Moore, in 1965, predicts technological progress and explains why the computer industry has been able to consistently come out with products that are smaller, more powerful, and less expensive than their predecessors) is that since you can buy a computer today that has twice as much storage space and completes transactions twice as fast as last year's model but will cost roughly half as much as it did last year, we expect the same efficiency from our organization's profit margin.

WHY LEADERSHIP MANAGEMENT?

Corporations are experiencing pressure to improve financial performance and return increased shareholder value. In markets where the opportunity to increase price is limited or nonexistent, companies have to look to their cost structures and operating methodologies to improve financial or revenue growth. The expectation is for them to realize the same scale profit margin in their organization's effectiveness model (consistently do more with less). In the same way that personal computers continue to evolve and are capable of doing more and more but cost less and less, our current business environment continues to depend on hi-tech gadgets and applications to perform the same or similar tasks that never quite seem to meet expectations.

Over the past few years, we have witnessed the worst business loss and economic downturn of this generation. In response, we are involved in a tremendous recovery effort in order to turn around the worst economic performance since the Great Depression. Lousy management, greed, and other errors caused this mess and will only be corrected by making huge changes in the way we manage leadership. We expected the managers we have performing our critical tasks will "do things right" and that our leaders will "do the right things." (Stephen R. Covey, author of *The 7 Habits of Highly Effective People*, says, "People and their managers are working so hard to be sure things are done right, that they hardly have time to decide if they are doing the right things.") Each organization has had to relook their processes and realign personnel in the midst of the high unemployment rates. Those employees that remain have increased output and "done more with less" but still more is required.

From the classroom to our health care system, to the grocery store, and including today's corporate workplace, the business of our business has become a war zone where we have to realize an ever-increasing ability to mine, manipulate, and manage data at increased speed but actually results in little to no sustainable increase in productivity. There has been a concept postulated that if all knowledge known to mankind could be quantified from the beginning of time until the wide-scale use of the computer somewhere in the 1960s that it collectively then doubled in capacity before the turn of the century and continues to double again every five years since that time and is increasing exponentially. We're much smarter in terms of sheer data points than we used to be, but if that's true, then why aren't we much wiser and increasingly more productive than we used to be? In fact, the opposite is true; we're spending more and more hours at work while achieving generally the same productivity levels. We now have cell phones, e-mail, Internet, Skype, Facebook, e-books, Twitter, and a host of other mediums and forms but don't seem to be able to communicate the really important things any better than we did before. Additionally, we aren't any happier with the results over time; in fact, the opposite is true. Also, the point has been made; these new forms of communication are not reliable or dependable. The point is that we can still read the Dead Sea Scrolls some two thousand years after they were written but are frightened we may lose priceless family photos if our computer crashes or the compact disc is played too many times.

While the tools we use continue to change over time, they remain just that—tools—which require the correct application and use to be effective. Many of us find it hard to remember what life was like before computers, e-mail, and cell phones. The transformation is nearly complete. In business meetings, classroom education, and even in the ways we worship, plasma has replaced chalkboard, and PowerPoint has become almost as prevalent in our society as television. We have witnessed, in only the last two decades, a complete change in the format of the way we communicate. Just as we saw the end of the record player when compact discs came out, casualties of this new and better means of communication system include the encyclopedia, the daily newspaper, the weekly magazines, the pencil with an eraser; and with the Kindle e-book, we will probably see the disappearance of bound books altogether soon. While this is interesting and a function of improvement over time, it comes at what cost? What are we missing in the transformation from writing with crushed wild berry ink with bird feather tips on animal skins to now reading and writing entire books entirely on a computer monitor? We use Google or other search engines to find information about any subject when we used to have to visit the library and look into the Dewey decimal system and search for a book. Just because we can incorporate additional tools and perform tasks much faster and easier doesn't mean we are asking and answering the correct questions.

Our need to communicate has not changed, just the tools we use to reach the target audience and the medium we choose to use in order to exchange information. Unfortunately, along with mass communication and efficiency sometimes comes sloppiness. With so much data available, we no longer appreciate how words are formed and sentences are structured. Robert Frost would invariably fail to entertain were he writing today simply because we have so many choices from which to get a weather report about "snow falling in the woods," for example. That age-old question reverberates—just because we can, does that mean we should? Has the pendulum swung too far in the wrong direction? Are we inundated with so much information that we have forgotten how to properly use the tools? We spend so much time answering e-mail notes and getting updates that no work is getting accomplished. We have access to the World Wide Web but fail to ask our coworkers how they are feeling or, more importantly, are they situationally aware of the changes needed to increase productivity. At times, we are in a roomful of people but feel like we have been abandoned and are on a deserted island.

I once worked for a man who refused to be a "slave" to e-mail. He told the five of us who were working for him that if we wanted to report anything to him or discuss any idea, we needed to schedule an appointment and do it face-to-face. He had his secretary print off anything that his boss sent to him so he could read it, and he would then dictate his response and have the secretary send it back if he had to send a response via e-mail. At first I thought he was crazy; then I realized he wasn't that far-off from the true course. I came to realize that what he missed in raw data, he made up for with reality. What he missed from a lack of speed and information, he made up for with accuracy and timing. He was a successful manager at the time because he used a hands-on approach. This manager was able to win the battle against the encroachment of technological gadgetry that seems to have invaded our culture.

An illustration of this principle was provided by a Chinese philosopher named Sun Tzu who lived around 500 BC. Though the tools of warfare at that time were swords and bow with arrows, the concepts presented by Sun Tzu have been used and valued most notably during the Vietnam War but are as current as today's headlines. The reason this is true is because Sun Tzu understood that it wasn't the tools of warfare that are most important but the overall vision and intent behind how the tools were used. He used the tools he needed to implement his plan and accomplish his overall objectives. He understood the importance of knowing how to apply the correct tools in order to accomplish a specific goal. As Sun Tzu quoted nearly two millennia ago, "If you know the enemy and know yourself, you need not fear the results of a hundred battles." Today, in the current industrial environment, our enemy is the proper use of time, and our battle is in understanding how best to use the fast-changing technological tools available to us. How many of us have preferred to send an e-mail rather than to make a phone call or log on rather than engage the workforce when what was really needed was a physical presence, leading by example, and thinking through the best solution rather than spraying the target with a machine gun approach?

There is a gap that has developed in our ability to process information. Over time, our technology has accepted the volume of information as a substitute for quality. There are a number of common focus areas that need to be addressed and investigated using the old-fashioned, time-tested way of doing business. This discussion will focus on these areas and provide a recommended manner of addressing each as appropriate. The tools used are not as important as the reason the process is being used. Along the way, an overarching principle will be applied wherever appropriate. It's called lean thinking and uses concepts first developed in the modern era by Henry Ford and others. It calls for the identification and elimination of waste and requires the hands-on approach to leadership. It maintains that the whole is greater than the cumulative addition sum of parts because there is a synergistic effect that takes place when individuals work together as a team. The process used and the methods that work better than others define the path forward. This discussion will focus on the how to manage assets and what tools seem to work better than others and explain what tools a manager needs to be successful. Rather than depending on the quality "process of the month," it will attempt to provide the blueprint for success to the manager looking to survive and even thrive on the technological battlefield that confronts us today.

The tools selected to express the concept of managing leadership, while effective, are not the primary focus area. There are proprietary intellectual property issues relating to these devices that will not be violated. The point of this discussion will not be to sell a specific process or methodology but rather to explain how best to set the conditions to use whatever tool seems best. Rather than trying to feed you each day so that you will keep coming back for more, this discussion will make an attempt to demonstrate how to use the "fishing pole" and will explain how best to "catch the fish" on your own so that you will see how the process should work and you can decide which "fishing pole" is best for your individual situation. The words of a fellow attendee at a major process improvement symposium continue to haunt when they said, "I understand how this works, and I see the relationship between the different levels and layers of supervision. What I'm missing is how to cause it all to happen." This discussion will show you the magic that is resident in today's industrial environment that will allow you to reign in all the technological advances and control data in order to execute and sustain effectiveness. The management of leadership will be accomplished by analyzing required pieces and parts common in each organization: communication (internally, externally, functionally), the management of change, compensation (how to define value in best business practices), project management (allocation of resources), human resources (how to recruit, train, sustain), leadership (the identification of common elements that lead to success), and the after-action review (how to learn from yourself); all while becoming lean and green throughout each process. Additional discussion will include working with unions (how to succeed without really trying) and how to recognize and mitigate organizational stress over time.

A recurring theme that will be used throughout is a concept developed by Norton and Kaplan, Harvard Business School, called balanced scorecard. *The balanced scorecard is a strategic planning and management system that is used extensively in business and industry, government, and nonprofit organizations worldwide to align business activities to the vision and strategy of the organization, improve internal and external communications, and monitor organization performance against strategic goals. It was originated by Drs. Robert Kaplan (Harvard Business School) and David Norton as a performance measurement framework that added strategic nonfinancial performance measures to traditional financial metrics to give managers and executives a more balanced view of organizational performance. While the phrase balanced scorecard was coined in the early 1990s, the roots of the this type of approach are deep and include the pioneering work of General Electric on performance measurement reporting in the 1950s and the work of French process engineers (who created the Tableau de Bord—literally, a "dashboard" of performance measures) in the early part of the twentieth century used to analyze organizations from different yet related perspectives.* The four views I will use (and explain in detail as examples) are as follows:

- **People:** the status or readiness of the organization, to perform a specific task including the current state of the facilities, the knowledge, skills and abilities, training, certification to perform all required tasks, etc., from a personnel standpoint. This area

WHY LEADERSHIP MANAGEMENT?

includes the use of information technology and how well you communicate internally and externally. The focus of this perspective answers the question: how are we enhancing the capabilities of our employees?

- **Process:** addresses the policies and procedures used to perform tasks for the product or services provided. Whether you are flying to the space station, making coffee, or changing a diaper, there is a process used to manage and integrate resources in sequence to achieve the desired result. This area focus answers the question: how can we improve the way work is performed in order to add value for our customer?
- **Product:** this area is concerned with the customer or perhaps how the shareholder views the value of the item produced or service provided. It is a validation of the contract and includes transparency, accountability, and efficiency. The focus of this perspective answers the question: what can we do to please our customer or how can we create value for our customer or shareholder?
- **Performance:** this addresses the rate or efficiency of the previous three areas: what does success look like, how are we achieving what our customer wants doing, and what can we do better? If we need to make changes in the types, amounts, and quality of resources, when should we do that? We can take a perceived weakness and turn it into strength depending on how many resources (man, material, method) we apply. Perhaps we should reinforce success or stop digging the hole deeper (wasting assets). Through regularly scheduled performance reviews, we can assess performance over time.

By answering these questions based on a critical view looking at our organization from these perspectives, we will be able to know where we are, have an idea how we are going to get there, and be able to adjust or react to changing conditions as necessary.

The "Becoming" Principle

Another recurring theme will be the "becoming" principle. The becoming principle is based on the concept that if you can think of or visualize the dream fulfilled and take steps that set the conditions to achieve that goal, it will happen. There are three actions that must be considered and then acted on for this concept to be realized as follows:

1. What do I need to do to develop my knowledge, skills, and abilities (what actions, training, study, resources, etc.) in order to be prepared to perform the task or assume the goal?
2. What actions need to happen by the small group of personnel that I interact with (family, work group, associates) need to accomplish in order for us to go from here to there?
3. How or what actions does my overall organizational culture need to take, look like, or become in order to reach the desired goal?

One of the most important questions to ask a young person is, where do you see yourself five years from now and what is it you are doing? How can I help you realize the person you want to become, and what do we need to do now, next year, and in subsequent years in order to get there? The becoming principle is a little bit like taking action to build a stone wall; you start by obtaining the brick and mortar, develop a plan for where you want to start and finish, then you begin laying a foundation by placing one stone upon another. The old joke on how does one eat an elephant is similar—one bite at a time.

How to Pick the Right Employees—Emotional Intelligence

This is a relatively new field of study that provides insight into how well an individual relates to others. It addresses the much-needed process of recruiting, hiring, training, and retaining the right employee. A consistent complaint across the board, in every industry, is that we now hire the résumé but put up with the individual. How many times have employers looked for and found the perfect fit for a particular position only to become painfully aware the chosen employee does not fit or isn't capable of performing the task he/she was hired for? Emotional intelligence is a fascinating field of study that tries to define and quantify why some people are able to accomplish success even though they don't score well on tests or, conversely, why some employees fail even though their résumés seemed perfect during the hiring process. Sometimes referred to as the "whole man" concept, emotional intelligence includes such nebulous terms as maturity, works well with others, has confidence, and self-confidence in his/her abilities. It attempts to define other aspects and characteristics of the human condition than test scores or graduate degrees. If all we wanted is a device to provide the right answer, we would design a machine capable of data mining answers for any and all questions. Another way of explaining it is to analyze why people who score really high on intelligence quotient tests sometimes fail at personal relationships. This discussion provides the missing piece we are all looking for when selecting prospective employees or the things the résumé won't tell you like: does this person get along well with others, is he/she a team player willing to work with others or only out for themselves, they may be really smart and technically proficient but are they able to translate that capability into action that can then be used? It's my experience there are four qualities or areas of a person's life that need to be evaluated and quantified that define and ensure balance in a person's life. These are the areas I am trying to determine when I look to hire a prospective employee.

- **Intelligence Quotient (IQ):** Is the person mentally capable of performing the task? Can he/she remember things they were taught, follow processes in a logical sequence, communicate effectively through written language, manipulate software programs (Microsoft word, Excel spreadsheets, PowerPoint, etc.) in order to provide information, have the experience required to effectively perform at the level that is required, etc.?

Too many times, this area dominates the résumé we are hiring, and we unfortunately hire brilliant fools who can come up with the right answers and know what they should have done but lack the ability to lead and manage or work with others in order to be successful.

- **Maturity Quotient (MQ):** It measures the maturity level of the individual. Basically, it answers the question whether the person fits the classic definition of maturity. "If you can keep your head when all about you are losing theirs and blaming it on you; If you can trust yourself when all men doubt you, but make allowance for their doubting too; . . . If you can meet with Triumph and Disaster and treat those two impostors just the same . . . yours is the Earth and everything that's in it" ([Joseph] Rudyard Kipling). Does this person overreact to every unexpected development or calmly work to correct or improve the situation is the question that I want to have answered through the hiring process.
- **Relational Quotient:** How does this person relate to others? Are they approachable, loyal, trusting, friendly, and maintain a positive outlook? I can think of some jobs where these qualities don't matter, but I expect them in a waitress and bell hop, and my customer expects them in the workforce I provide them when I perform services on their products. In the hiring process, how do I determine what's real and what's imagined? How good a judge of character are the hiring managers I have recruiting our workforce? Basically, I want individuals who are sincere and capable of adding value and developing favor with others.
- **Spiritual Quotient: It** is a measure that looks at a person's belief system in the same way intelligence quotient looks at cognitive intelligence. It is the study of the following areas of an individual's personality: honesty, integrity, artistic potential, realist view, and conventional/unconventional approach to philosophical belief system. While this area is harder to define, it may be the most important of all areas in many respects and has become a major focus area for employee development in many industries.

WHY LEADERSHIP MANAGEMENT?

Ethics, compliance, and the rule of law in the workplace have become critically important as cases of infidelity continue to make headlines. Since it is easier to hire honest employees than try to teach morality, this should be a major focus area in the hiring process. I am not aware of any individual who is able to turn on or off moral turpitude at will. While it may be possible for people who are trying to "do the right thing" to slip and fall occasionally, I am not aware of anyone who intentionally fails in the areas of honesty, integrity, and morality to suddenly become the model citizen.

When employers initiate reviews of prospective employees, what is needed is a checklist of questions that allows an appropriate evaluation of the individual being considered. It should be a type of Myers-Briggs Personality Assessment test that provides a scoring of each of the areas described above before the individual is selected. Rather than leaving such critical areas left to chance, these questions should be answered—how many positions and how many different jobs has the individual had in the past ten years? Has the individual moved around a lot or listed too many accomplishments? What caused these moves? Where does the individual think he will be working and at what level in the next five years? Depending on the type of job being considered, these and other answers are required and can save a lot of time over the long-term if the hiring process takes them into account. Like all special tools, we need to be calibrated to a specific standard in order to be useful for a specific purpose.

Personal Experience and Hands-on Approach

The list of tools provided in this discussion are those that I personally have tried and know function properly. I recently applied for and was certified as a project management professional by the Project Management Institute (PMP number 1228271). In the process of obtaining this accreditation, I was focused on the many times I have worked on, been responsible for, or associated with management concepts and applications. These examples of previous accomplishments exhibit both hands-on as well as teaching and coaching experience, which I feel is a prerequisite for working with and communicating to any group when addressing management and process improvement. These experiences and others provided the preparation needed to see the importance of being an active participant in any discussion concerning change management, process improvement, communication, process integration, and resource allocation and application.

The current business environment that describes our industrial, administrative, governmental, and/or personal services contractual relationships continue to change over time. We will always have tools that make tasks easier and more efficient than previous methods. What doesn't change is the way these tools are applied and how we manage them and lead our personnel to accomplish required tasks. Leadership management is the magic that makes it happen by correctly applying the processes and procedures that have worked over time, by managing leadership.

Lean Six Sigma Process Improvement

This concept has been around for decades arguably as early as Henry Ford's Model A automobile manufacturing process. It has been further developed by others including Toyota, MIT, Motorola, and others. The basic concept is to identify and eliminate the waste that exists in the various processes any organization uses to produce products and services. Originally developed in assembly line manufacturing activities, it has recently branched out to other areas including finance, health care, education, human resource acquisition, and all other areas where two or more individuals use recurring processes and procedures. Contrary to popular opinion, it is not strictly a quality control or quality assurance focused effort but more a mind-set on how to increase efficiency and become better at what you are trying to do.

WHY LEADERSHIP MANAGEMENT?

Inherent in Lean Six Sigma Process Improvement concept is facilitating the individual employees or members of the group to identify where improvement is needed and how best to cause improvement to be achieved and sustained. Those organizations that have been most successful spend the time and effort (application of resources) to communicate within the group and encourage total participation. Senior management support and interest is absolutely critical. In the same way, the responsibility of parenting your children cannot be delegated or assigned to a substitute; senior management must be personally involved in all Lean Six Sigma initiatives. The boss can't do it himself, but he/she must demonstrate its importance to all participants. Without senior management support and interest, LSS becomes just another flavor of the month.

No. 1 Moore's law *is a term actually associated from an observation made by Intel cofounder Gordon Moore in 1965, which states that while the capability of a computer will double its capability, the cost associated with purchasing the newest computer will decrease by half. In other words, if you buy a computer today that has a 250-megabyte storage capacity for $1,000, you will be able to purchase its equivalent model in eighteen months that has twice the capacity (500 megabytes) for half the price ($500). This trend continues for the most part throughout the information technology industry.*

CHAPTER ONE

COMMUNICATION (OUR MOST IMPORTANT YET LEAST UNDERSTOOD) PROCESS

Managing Change in Communication Planning

In today's fast-paced culture, we are inundated with information from every aspect of society. In the past thirty years, we have witnessed a fundamental change in the way data is collected, transmitted, assembled, turned into information, formulated through different mediums, and communicated as wisdom. For thousands of years, mankind recorded information by scratching forms onto rock, paper, wood, and any other material available using rocks, ink, and other writing implements. Beginning around the time when Ben Franklin identified the electronic pulse in electricity, we have continued to learn how to manage and control electricity and use it to communicate as an energy source initially by sending it along a wire and then through the air to anywhere we wanted. About a hundred years ago, we learned how to use the telegraph; thirty years ago, if you wanted to correspond with someone, you could write a letter, call them on the telephone, send a cable, read about them in the newspaper, or watch them on television. Today, one is able to communicate in real time to just about anywhere including under the sea and up to and including the moon in any number of ways and means. The change that has taken place has virtually eliminated the need for daily newspapers, pencils, and recently, those devices that can only be used as phones or only as a camera (rather than a combination phone, typewriter, facsimile transmitter, navigation system, camera, and computer system that fits in your pocket).

The resource that has been most affected by our newly developed communication tool technology is our use of time. Even though we can stream live video on our laptop while talking to the other side of the world on our cell phone, working a crossword puzzle while watching television or travelling cross-country in a plane, train, or automobile doesn't mean we should. Using the analogy of how rules and tools impact driving a car through traffic, we need rules to follow so we can all travel on the highways at the same time. People who like to drive probably don't like stop signs, speed limits on highways, or any rule that impedes them, but we all acknowledge that these rules of the road are necessary tools so that we can all operate at the same time on the roads safely. Tools and rules are necessary for us to communicate effectively among ourselves too.

The use of these and other tools have to be learned and managed to be properly applied in our everyday lives. As we learn to use them, we also have to develop a methodology or commonly understood rules and regulations so we can quickly and easily understand one another. Take electronic mail, or e-mail, for example; rules have developed over time to help guide and manage how we send e-mail messages. These commonsense rules have changed slightly over time with the addition of new types of communication: e-mail, texting, Skype, Facebook, etc., but basically have remained the same.

E-mail Etiquette: Rules to Govern Office Communication

1. **Be concise and to the point.**
   Do not make an e-mail longer than it needs to be. Remember that reading an e-mail is harder than reading printed communications;

LEADERSHIP MANAGEMENT TOOLBOX

and a long e-mail can be very discouraging to read, but don't leave out important details that will help your recipient answer your query.

2. **Answer all questions and preempt further questions.**
   An e-mail reply must answer all questions and preempt further questions—if you do not answer all the questions in the original e-mail, you will receive further e-mails regarding the unanswered questions, which will not only waste your time and your customer's time but also cause considerable frustration. Moreover, if you are able to preempt relevant questions, your customer will be grateful and impressed with your efficient and thoughtful customer service. Imagine, for instance, that a customer sends you an e-mail asking which credit cards you accept. Instead of just listing the credit card types, you can guess that their next question will be about how they can order, so you also include some order information and a URL to your order page. Customers will definitely appreciate this.

3. **Use proper spelling, grammar, and punctuation.**
   This is not only important because improper spelling, grammar, and punctuation give a bad impression of your company, it is also important for conveying the message properly. E-mails with no full stops or commas are difficult to read and can sometimes even change the meaning of the text. And if your program has a spell-checking option, why not use it? While you can write in a conversational tone (contractions are okay), pay attention to basic rules of grammar.

4. **Make it personal.**
   Not only should the e-mail be personally addressed, it should also include personal or customized content. For this reason, auto replies are usually not very effective. However, templates can be used effectively in this way. See next tip.

COMMUNICATION

5. **Use templates for frequently used responses.**
   Some questions you get over and over again, such as directions to your office or how to subscribe to your newsletter. Save these texts as response templates and paste these into your message when you need them. You can save your templates in a Word document or use preformatted e-mails.

6. **Answer swiftly.**
   Customers send an e-mail because they wish to receive a quick response. If they did not want a quick response, they would send a letter or a fax. Therefore, each e-mail should be replied to within at least twenty-four hours and preferably within the same working day. If the e-mail is complicated, just send an e-mail back saying that you have received it and that you will get back to them. This will put the customer's mind at rest, and usually, customers will then be very patient!

7. **Do not attach unnecessary files.**
   By sending large attachments, you can annoy customers and even bring down their e-mail system. Wherever possible, try to compress attachments and only send attachments when they are productive. Moreover, you need to have a good virus scanner in place since your customers will not be very happy if you send them documents full of viruses!

8. **Use proper structure and layout.**
   Since reading from a screen is more difficult than reading from paper, the structure and layout is very important for e-mail messages. Use short paragraphs and blank lines between each paragraph. When making points, number them or mark each point as separate to keep the overview.

9. **Do not overuse the high-priority option.**
   We all know the story of the boy who cried wolf. If you overuse the high-priority option, it will lose its function when you really need it.

Moreover, even if a mail has high priority, your message will come across as slightly aggressive if you flag it as high priority.

10. **Do not write in CAPITALS.**
    IF YOU WRITE IN CAPITALS, IT SEEMS AS IF YOU ARE SHOUTING. This can be highly annoying and might trigger an unwanted response in the form of a flame mail. Therefore, try not to send any e-mail text in capitals.

11. **Don't leave out the message thread.**
    When you reply to an e-mail, you must include the original mail in your reply; in other words, click Reply instead of New Mail. Some people say that you must remove the previous message since this has already been sent and is, therefore, unnecessary. However, I could not agree less. If you receive many e-mails, you obviously cannot remember each individual e-mail. This means that a threadless e-mail will not provide enough information, and you will have to spend a frustratingly long time to find out the context of the e-mail in order to deal with it. Leaving the thread might take a fraction longer in download time, but it will save the recipient much more time and frustration in looking for the related e-mails in their inbox!

12. **Add disclaimers to your e-mails.**
    It is important to add disclaimers to your internal and external mails since this can help protect your company from liability. Consider the following scenario: An employee accidentally forwards a virus to a customer by e-mail. The customer decides to sue your company for damages. If you add a disclaimer at the bottom of every external mail, saying that the recipient must check each e-mail for viruses and that it cannot be held liable for any transmitted viruses, this will surely be of help to you in court (read more about *e-mail disclaimers*). Another example: an employee sues the company for allowing a racist e-mail to circulate

the office. If your company has an *e-mail policy* in place and adds an e-mail disclaimer to every mail that states that employees are expressly required not to make defamatory statements, you have a good case of proving that the company did everything it could to prevent offensive e-mails.

13. **Read the e-mail before you send it.**
A lot of people don't bother to read an e-mail before they send it out as can be seen from the many spelling and grammar mistakes contained in e-mails. Apart from this, reading your e-mail through the eyes of the recipient will help you send a more effective message and avoid misunderstandings and inappropriate comments.

14. **Do not overuse Reply to All.**
Only use Reply to All if you really need your message to be seen by each person who received the original message.

15. **Mailings—use the Bcc: field or do a mail merge.**
When sending an e-mail mailing, some people place all the e-mail addresses in the To: field. There are two drawbacks to this practice: (1) the recipient knows that you have sent the same message to a large number of recipients, and (2) you are publicizing someone else's e-mail address without their permission. One way to get round this is to place all addresses in the Bcc: field. However, the recipient will only see the address from the To: field in their e-mail, so if this was empty, the To: field will be blank and this might look like spamming. You could include the mailing list e-mail address in the To: field; or even better, if you have Microsoft Outlook and Word, you can do a mail merge and create one message for each recipient. A mail merge also allows you to use fields in the message so that you can, for instance, address each recipient personally. For more information on how to do a Word mail merge, consult the Help in Word.

LEADERSHIP MANAGEMENT TOOLBOX

16. **Take care with abbreviations and emoticons.**
    In business e-mails, try not to use abbreviations such as BTW (by the way) and LOL (laugh out loud). The recipient might not be aware of the meanings of the abbreviations, and in business e-mails, these are generally not appropriate. The same goes for emoticons, such as the smiley :-). If you are not sure whether your recipient knows what it means, it is better not to use it.

17. **Be careful with formatting.**
    Remember that when you use formatting in your e-mails, the sender might not be able to view formatting or might see different fonts than you had intended. When using colors, use a color that is easy to read on the background.

18. **Take care with rich text and HTML messages.**
    Be aware that when you send an e-mail in rich text or HTML format, the sender might only be able to receive plain text e-mails. If this is the case, the recipient will receive your message as a .txt attachment. Most e-mail clients, however, including Microsoft Outlook, are able to receive HTML and rich text messages.

19. **Do not forward chain letters.**
    Do not forward chain letters. We can safely say that all of them are hoaxes. Just delete the letters as soon as you receive them.

20. **Do not request delivery and read receipts.**
    This will almost always annoy your recipient before he or she has even read your message. Besides, it usually does not work anyway since the recipient could have blocked that function or his/her software might not support it, so what is the use of using it? If you want to know whether an e-mail was received, it is better to ask the recipient to let you know if it was received.

COMMUNICATION

21. **Do not ask to recall a message.**
    Biggest chances are that your message has already been delivered and read. A recall request would look very silly in that case, wouldn't it? It is better just to send an e-mail to say that you have made a mistake. This will look much more honest than trying to recall a message.

22. **Do not copy a message or attachment without permission.**
    Do not copy a message or attachment belonging to another user without permission of the originator. If you do not ask permission first, you might be infringing on copyright laws.

23. **Do not use e-mail to discuss confidential information.**
    Sending an e-mail is like sending a postcard. If you don't want your e-mail to be displayed on a bulletin board, don't send it. Moreover, never make any libelous, sexist, or racially discriminating comments in e-mails even if they are meant to be a joke.

24. **Use a meaningful subject.**
    Try to use a subject that is meaningful to the recipient as well as yourself. For instance, when you send an e-mail to a company requesting information about a product, it is better to mention the actual name of the product (e.g., product A information) than to just say "product information" or the company's name in the subject.

25. **Use active instead of passive.**
    Try to use the active voice of a verb wherever possible. For instance, "We will process your order today" sounds better than "Your order will be processed today." The first sounds more personal, whereas the latter, especially when used frequently, sounds unnecessarily formal.

26. **Avoid using URGENT and IMPORTANT.**
    Even more so than the high-priority option, you must, at all times, try to avoid these types of words in an e-mail or subject line. Only use this if it is a really, really urgent or important message.

LEADERSHIP MANAGEMENT TOOLBOX

27. **Avoid long sentences.**
    Try to keep your sentences to a maximum of fifteen to twenty words. E-mail is meant to be a quick medium and requires a different kind of writing than letters. Also, take care not to send e-mails that are too long. If a person receives an e-mail that looks like a dissertation, chances are that they will not even attempt to read it!

28. **Don't send or forward e-mails containing libelous, defamatory, offensive, racist, or obscene remarks.** By sending or even just forwarding one libelous or offensive remark in an e-mail, you and your company can face court cases resulting in multimillion dollar penalties.

29. **Don't forward virus hoaxes and chain letters.**
    If you receive an e-mail message warning you of a new unstoppable virus that will immediately delete everything from your computer, this is most probably a hoax. By forwarding hoaxes, you use valuable bandwidth, and sometimes virus hoaxes contain viruses themselves by attaching a so-called file that will stop the dangerous virus. The same goes for chain letters that promise incredible riches or ask your help for a charitable cause. Even if the content seems to be bona fide, the senders are usually not. Since it is impossible to find out whether a chain letter is real or not, the best place for it is the recycle bin.

30. **Keep your language gender neutral.**
    In this day and age, avoid using sexist language such as "The user should add a signature by configuring his e-mail program." Apart from using he/she, you can also use the neutral gender "The user should add a signature by configuring the e-mail program."

31. **Don't reply to spam.**
    By replying to spam or by unsubscribing, you are confirming that your e-mail address is live. Confirming this will only generate even more spam. Therefore, just hit the Delete button or use an e-mail software to remove spam automatically.

COMMUNICATION

32. **Use Cc: field sparingly.**
    Try not to use the Cc: field unless the recipient in the Cc: field knows why they are receiving a copy of the message. Using the Cc: field can be confusing since the recipients might not know who is supposed to act on the message. Also, when responding to a Cc: message, should you include the other recipient in the Cc: field as well? This will depend on the situation. In general, do not include the person in the Cc: field unless you have a particular reason for wanting this person to see your response. Again, make sure that this person will know why they are receiving a copy.

33. **Mind your manners.**
    Think of the basic rules you learned growing up, like saying please and thank you. Address people you don't know as Mr., Mrs., or Dr. Only address someone by first name if they imply it's okay to do so.

34. **Watch your tone.**
    A dictionary defines *tone* as an "accent or inflection expressive of a mood or emotion." It is very difficult to express tone in writing. You want to come across as respectful, friendly, and approachable. You don't want to sound curt or demanding.

35. **Be professional.**
    This means, stay away from abbreviations and don't use emoticons (those little smiley faces). Don't use a cute or suggestive e-mail address for business communications.

36. **Wait to fill in the TO e-mail address.**
    Never fill in the TO e-mail address until completely through proofing e-mail and sure that it is exactly the way that you want it. This will keep you from accidentally sending an e-mail prematurely. In the past, accidentally clicking on the send icon, when you really meant to click on the attachment icon, could be a big mistake.

As e-mail developed over time and has now become the mainstream interoffice means of communicating, it, by necessity, became the official means of recording messages. It wasn't that long ago that business culture refused to accept e-mail messages as legal, binding forms of communication. If it wasn't written down on paper and signed, it didn't count. Through transformational evolution, we learned to adapt as we went from having to print off a document we had typed onto our computer screens in order to be able to see what we had written; eventually society began feeling more comfortable, making changes on the computer screen itself. Because we could make changes and there was more capability (change font, size, spacing, cut-and-paste copying, etc.) on the screen without having to "kill a tree" over and over again, we learned to manage document communication using a new medium. This led to a series of new capabilities, including a newly discovered risk associated with use of a cell phone or texting our friends while driving. Studies have found that the poor weak-minded human being is incapable of driving and texting or using a cell phone at the same time; driving while texting is equivalent to driving while intoxicated or under the influence and carries stiff penalties in some states. Who would have thought this problem would present itself even two decades ago? As capabilities continue to evolve rules and, in some cases, laws, it will have to be adapted to fit the new methodologies.

Any military historian will tell you that one of the most important inventions of its time was the stirrup for the horse saddle. In and of itself, it may not look like much, but because it set the conditions for stabilizing a mounted warrior on horseback as he maneuvered across the battlefield, it led to significant change in how warfare was conducted. The change that took place in the relatively recent past in the way society communicates came about haphazardly almost by accident but still needs to be managed. In the same way that society learned to cope with the introduction of the printing press, the telegraph line, wireless communication, and television, managers need to learn how to use these communication tools to manage the Internet, exchange data, and cause information to become wisdom.

Communications Planning Structure

The matrix below defines a simple process that can be used to define and take inventory of how your organization communicates. It's not just a matter of what you say; you need this structure in order to set the conditions to allow other mechanisms to take effect. Communications planning involves six major phases or dimensions to be considered are the following:

- Medium (channel, format, type of delivery system)
- Primary target (audience, destination, receiver, to whom message sent)
- Content (what type of information presented)
- Delivery method (verbal, televised, newsprint, e-mail, etc.)
- Frequency of message (reinforcement)
- Responsibility (who owns and controls the message?)

Planning matrix for managing communications through a communication plan

Medium	Primary Audience	Type of Information Presented	Delivery Method	Delivery Frequency	Who is Responsible? Who OWNS the process?
Information System, Newsletter	Hourly Employees	Current Status Of contract	Internet Explorer	Daily	Management

The *medium* is the how you choose to present the information. In the same way an advertisement agency looks at new and unique ways to present information (such as banners on city buses, posters hanging on the walls, and commercials), management can use subtle methods to focus attention on key concepts. Examples of success stories include weekly safety meetings before work begins, newsletters, screen savers, town hall sessions with all employees, to name a few. This area is limited only by your imagination.

LEADERSHIP MANAGEMENT TOOLBOX

The *primary target audience* is perhaps the most complex concept to understand in communications planning. Basically, it's "who are you trying to reach with this specific message?" Senior management needs to understand this concept and focus resources like a laser beam in order to be effective. A simple example used to explain it is named dirty bathroom. The idea is that there always seems to be a paper towel mess inside the men's bathroom at a particular workplace. Management decides they want to send a message encouraging everyone to clean as they go. The target audience is those male persons working on that floor that use that bathroom. You don't want to waste anyone's attention or any resources by posting signs at the main entrance to the factory, on other floors, or to anyone not using that bathroom (like female employees, for example). The same is true if you are trying to get the attention of the supply clerks, hourly personnel, students, teachers, management, janitors, all newly hired employees, etc. You need to understand what the message is and who needs to receive it and then plan accordingly.

The *type of information presented* seems easy to understand but oftentimes surprises management in its simplicity. Most employees have simple questions they should not have to spend a lot of time finding answers to. Basically, their primary interests are in three general areas:

1. Current status: how the organization is doing
2. WIIFM (what's in it for me) in terms of compensation, future options, and
3. What is coming up in the near term that will impact me?

Information about specific areas of the company that are doing well or human interest stories will garner attention, but planning needs to "scratch the itch," answer the primary questions most important to all employees.

The *delivery method* defines how the message is delivered. It could be verbally, via e-mail, on a poster, in a newsletter, or all of the above. Some

COMMUNICATION

of us pay more attention when someone is speaking to us; others do better seeing the message written out with photos. The best message ever created is worthless if it's not delivered or not properly received.

The *delivery frequency* is the number of times the message needs to be transmitted. A wise old man once told me that a message needs to be transmitted seven times for a human being to remember it. Another adage states that you have the tendency to remember things that you have experienced for a year but tend to lose detail after that time frame. The frequency required is determined by subject complexity and importance.

The *process owner* is the individual designated to manage the communication plan. Usually this individual is also authorized to apply resources to ensure effective communication takes place.

Communications Plan (Getting the Word Out)

Task Organization: Managers, Assigned Personnel

1. **Purpose:** to establish a unified process whereby all internal communication is planned, coordinated, directed, and controlled using all tools available.
2. **Intent:** provide a method of sharing information that is easily understood to the workforce in a standardized manner.
3. **Situation:**

    a. General: As information changes over time and new concepts are developed and introduced, the requirement exists to inform employees and ensure understanding and process compliance. In order to ensure message integrity and consistency, this communications plan will prioritize resources and establish a coordinated process that facilitates the dissemination of key messages and critical information.

b. Environment: The workplace environment is such that attempts to provide formal communication products, and brief process changes are restricted by space and time. With an already-filled work schedule, the time allotted to communicate on the flight line, the shop floor, or in the hangar with all employees, though vital for success, is often restricted or abbreviated. In order to be effective, the discussions must be short, to the point, and easily understood by everyone.

c. Vision: This framework provides a process that explains how our company, school, or organization will communicate with all individuals. In order to manage change, we will utilize a change management process that incorporates *awareness* of the change, *desire* to make the change possible, *knowledge* and skill levels for what the change represents, what *abilities* will be required to accomplish the change, and then a *reinforcement* plan to repeat the message as necessary to ensure (ADKAR) techniques. By identifying the key message, the target audience, and the transmission medium and frequency and assigning task responsibility, the communication process will begin. As the process continues, it will be modified and improved. Most importantly, it is essential the target audience is provided the "what's in it for me" (WIIFM) concept. This major focus point will increase buy-in and awareness of concepts and ideas.

4. **Goal:** In coordination with all other areas, managers, and directorates, this process will plan, coordinate, direct, and control all key communication processes, methods, and mediums (to include newsletter articles, written word, informational briefings, television broadcasts, use of the Internet and web sites, posters, and other ways of getting the word out). Included in this effort will be assigning ownership, defining responsibilities, establishing time lines, developing phased goals and objectives, allocating resources, and ensuring approval of the program director.

COMMUNICATION

5. **Execution:** Each senior leader will develop a communications plan and submit for coordination and to the director for approval. The following elements should be addressed by each scorecard holder:

Key Message: A simple statement of fact that provides relevance to each member of the target audience. Each program element should be focused and easily understood.

Intent: After receiving the above message, every employee understands key concept changes, purpose, and the role they play in meeting contract requirements. It is anticipated that we will use everything available from simple tri-fold handout documents to posters to group briefings to one-on-one discussions throughout the contract. Additionally, PowerPoint briefings, films, and other information formats could be placed on the internal web site, via other means, etc.

Target Audience(s): Who is the individual, group, or work center that is receiving the message? Does the message have to be pushed (briefed, displayed, or delivered with follow-up action to ensure understanding), or can it be expected the information will be pulled (will the intended audience grasp it on their own without being directed to them)?

Goal(s): With stated objectives and considering available human and financial resources, define program or process of work for each medium (see attachments). Goals include general programs, products, or services used to achieve stated objectives. For example, if the objective is to improve customer satisfaction, goals might include meeting and exceeding contract requirements, improving training and KSA for our employees, enhancing communications, etc. The intent is to translate goals and objectives throughout the organization with emphasis on the lowest levels.

LEADERSHIP MANAGEMENT TOOLBOX

Time line: Once objectives, goals, audiences, and tools have been identified, specific times, places, dates (to include reinforcement initiatives) will be established that outlines each program so as to facilitate synchronization, integration, and staff coordination. Ensure translation into Spanish is taken into account.

First-Line Supervisor Focus: This information is designed to explain how the information could be organized to enhance buy-in for the communications plan. In order to effectively communicate, the focus must begin with the first-line supervisor. The proper allocation of resources (training, time, material, format, etc.) must be provided also.

Individual Acceptance and Buy-In: The intended message for this audience will require extensive coordination and planning. Since most of the workforce may be averse to change, the information will have to be pushed to them rather than expecting them to pull the information from the various programs on their own.

6. **Service and Supply Support Needed:** In addition to supplies and materials, there is a requirement to use IT tools such as projectors, plotters (to make posters), sharing space on the hangar walls, and expanding other capabilities such as information pamphlets, etc. This portion of the communications plan requires detailed planning depending on the type medium supported.

   For Coordination:

   - Training Communications appendix
   - Human Resources Communications appendix
   - Safety Communications appendix
   - Country Team Communications appendix

COMMUNICATION

A Different Way of Communicating

The way we communicate internally as an organization requires planning and organization. In a typical organization, regularly scheduled gatherings take place (sometimes called staff call) or just weekly meeting. Most of these events begin with the leader announcing what decisions have been made or the overall guidance and direction that will be taken in the upcoming time frame. This is followed normally by the custom of asking for individuals to comment on their area of expertise going around the room. This form of exchanging information has not changed in probably ten thousand years. One can picture a group of cavemen sitting around a campfire discussing how hungry they were and planning how they were going to go out and find food. In modern day, with the communication tools we have now, there needs to be a different way of exchanging data, information, and wisdom. The most precious commodity we have is time. In order to make the best use of it, there is an evolution that must take place in any group of people. Using the caveman example, after the first few meetings, the leader would demand that all hunters come to the meeting prepared to discuss that portion they are going to contribute. For example, you would expect the guy who was sent out to find where the animals are to be ready to give the group that information; the guy who makes the spears should be able to tell the chief how many spears are on hand, the guy who is in charge of processing the meat would be ready to tell each member where he is to bring it once they have found it, and so on. Each member needs to have properly prepared themselves prior to the meeting session. The group needs to be organized and use tools to manage processes and procedures to save time.

Today's business meetings or staff calls are similar in nature and now require managing in a different manner. Rather than "going around the table," asking what each member has to contribute, it saves time if the leader assigns ownership for focus areas for each process so that each "process owner" is held responsible and accountable for each particular task or effort. Where others have input to a particular process they join in.

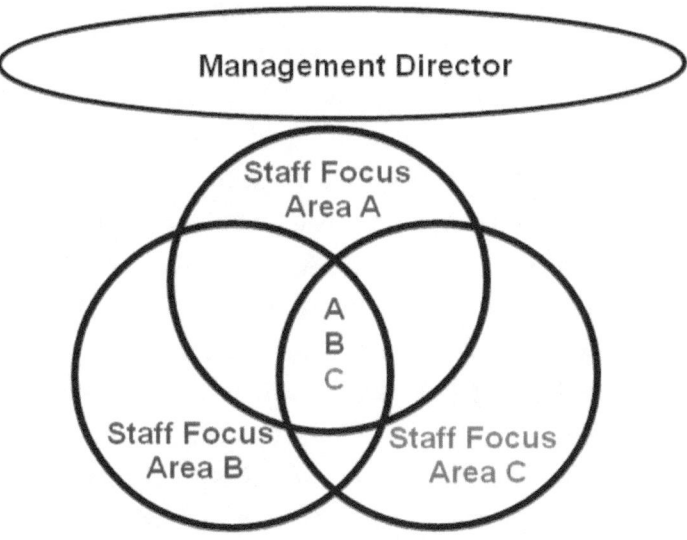

In this way, tools would be used effectively and all members of the group would be allowed to contribute. Time management is critical to communications management.

The benefit to the difference in the two processes is that by assigning a process owner, a tremendous amount of time is saved. The "laser beam" focus primarily on the most important things going on in the organization prevents confusion on the part of all participants concerning priorities and what is most important. Even the most knowledgeable and most experienced managers sometimes lose focus on what the boss (or perhaps the customer) feels are the most important things that require attention and subsequent action. This process takes time to establish and requires reinforcement (to prevent wandering back into the old ways of doing business) but can provide exceptional results. Are you having two-hour meetings that seem to only rehash what was talked about the previous week? This is a possible solution. The staff will reflect the personality and intentions of the boss either directly or unintentionally.

The Impact of Life's Experiences on Communication with Different Age-Groups

In his book, *The People Puzzle, Understanding Yourself and Others*, Morris Massey suggests that we are all programmed in much the same way one would program a computer. The information input consists of eight separate categories of sources of programming experiences, which range from the impact of family influence to geographical location. When we are confronted by a given set of circumstances, we are forced to react in a set manner. A simplistic example of Massey's theory of programming would be to explain the cause-and-effect relationship between how parents raise a child and how that child acts as an adult. The small child is playing with a toy and accidentally breaks it. The parents, thinking they are comforting the child, fix the problem by buying the child a new toy identical to the first. As the child continues to grow, the parents anticipate him breaking each new toy, so they automatically purchase two toys each time they go to the store. The child never learns the concept that once a toy breaks, then it's gone. As he grows to manhood, he becomes accustomed to his parents fixing all problems. He breaks whatever he likes, and the parents take care of it for him. If he breaks the fifty-five-miles-per-hour speed limit, it doesn't matter because the parents will correct the problem for him. Massey goes on to explain that reprogramming can occur after what he terms a significant emotional event (SEE) takes place. This is an event that is so mentally arresting that it forces the individual to examine and change his value standard. An example of reprogramming might be the indoctrination process an individual goes through during basic training in the military or experiencing a terrible accident, etc. Massey points out many influences that affect different groups of people. Examples of influences that affected large groups of people collectively were the Great Depression, Prohibition, Dr. Spock, Watergate, etc. Those of us who experienced the Kennedy assassination and 9/11 can remember where we were and what we were doing when those events took place.

Massey illustrates his point about recognizing subtle differences in people by citing the example of an assembly line manager whose workforce was composed of various different age-groups of personnel. He had both older and younger employees who had differing life experiences (were programmed differently) working on an assembly line producing a set product. Through trial and error the manager found in order to distribute effective rewards and punishment for good and bad behavior (for minor infractions like coming to work late or taking too long at breaks), he had to punish different people in different ways. The only option the manager had was to cause the errant worker to either not come to work during the normal work week or to make the employee come in during the weekend. The manager found the loss of salary for not coming to work or the added money received for working longer hours had very little impact whatsoever. Eventually, he discovered that by directing the older set of employees to not come to work on a normal workday had the same effect as causing the younger generation to have to work on the weekends. The manager determined in order to punish the older group who had been influenced by the Great Depression by preventing them from coming to work during a normal workday caused them to feel so guilty that he only had to threaten to impose punishment afterward to achieve the desired result. The same tactic used on the younger generation, however, had the opposite effect. In fact, this group welcomed the unexpected holiday. The manager found that making the younger generation employee come to work on the weekend to make up for lost work significantly inconvenienced the younger employee. There was the issue of loss of pay, etc., but the impact wasn't felt until pay day, which was at the end of the month, so the effect was minimalized. So in effect, the manager managed his personnel differently based on their age-group (how they had been programmed to respond to change in work schedule). The point is that both groups had been programmed to respond differently based on their own set of values that had evolved from childhood. Unless we experience a SEE, we react to influences in our environment as we have been programmed.

The older individual, with few exceptions, would like to maintain a traditionalist role for females. The younger generation, however, being exposed to a different set of circumstances, is more willing to accept the female as an equal member of the team. Massey has provided a logical explanation for the generation gap in our society. This is the way I see society as a whole in terms of the perception of the role of females in the military.

Susan Hannam and Bonni Yordi, working with the IBM Center for the Business of Government, published an extensive report that explains and defines the different ways people of different age-groups see things and react to them. In *Engaging a Multi-Generational Workforce: Practical Advice for Government Managers,* Susan Hannam and Bonni Yordi establish four distinct generational groups:

- *Traditionalists*, age sixty-six and older, born between 1922 and 1945
- *Boomers*, age forty-seven to sixty-five, born between 1946 and 1964
- *Gen Xers*, age thirty-one to forty-six, born between 1965 and 1980
- *Millennials*, age twenty-one to thirty, born between 1981 and 1990

In a fascinating discussion, the IBM Center report outlines the transition taking place in the workplace today (2011) and outline both the challenges and opportunities that exist in the process of explaining the specific differences and suggestions for communicating with each generation.

Traditionalists

Preferred methods of communication:
- Memos
- Letters
- Personal notes
- Individual interactions

Suggested ways to communicate:
- Words and tone of voice should be respectful, with good grammar, clear diction, no slang or profanity.
- Language should be formal and professional, and the message should relate to organization history and long-term goals.

Boomers

Preferred methods of communication:
- Face-to-face
- Phone calls
- Personal interaction
- Structured networking

Suggested ways to communicate:
- Conversations should be more informal, perhaps over coffee or lunch.
- Boomers tend to see relationship and business results as intertwined. Ask about mutual interests (e.g., "How is your son doing in college?").
- Make the conversation interactive by getting the other's input and link the message to the team or individual vision, mission, and values.

Gen Xers

Preferred methods of communication:
- Voice mail
- E-mail
- Casual
- Direct and immediate

Suggested ways to communicate:
- Don't waste the Gen Xer's time. Be direct and straightforward.
- Avoid corporate speak.

COMMUNICATION

- Send an e-mail or leave a voice mail that clearly states what you want, how it will serve the Gen Xer, and when you want it.

Millennials

Preferred methods of communication:
- Digital (instant messages, blogs, text messages)
- Collaborative interaction

Suggested ways to communicate:
- Be positive.
- Send a text message or meet face-to-face.
- Tie the message to the millennial's personal goals or to goals the entire team is working toward.
- Don't be condescending.
- Avoid cynicism and sarcasm.

The report is a "must read" for all managers because it provides a long list of tools, processes, and procedures that could enhance any organization. Anything that improves our most important yet least understood process of managing our employees is vital to success.

CHAPTER TWO

DEFINING AND GUIDING LEADERSHIP

Believe it or not, our employees/coworkers/friends/family/associates are historically the most underutilized and mismanaged group we will ever come in contact with. The groups of people we have, providing supervision and leadership for these employees, usually aren't properly trained, basically aren't told what to expect, and, more importantly, what's expected from them. We don't give them the tools they need to communicate well enough with one another and usually don't allow them to develop the tools they need to become successful. Even though many of us have identified the problem, there simply aren't meaningful, useful tools available out there to fix the problem.

The reason tools aren't widely used is obvious, but ways to develop corrective actions are not well understood. In the current business environment, we usually "hire the résumé" and deal with the individual's capabilities after he/she comes to work. We inevitably expect previous experience to be a qualifier for successful performance without even communicating vision, goals, expectations, and defining what success looks like. In the same way, we expect a sporting coach to just know how to train, motivate, and correctly make decisions about how to win the big game, we expect managers to just know what shareholders are thinking and consider to be the most important areas to focus

DEFINING AND GUIDING LEADERSHIP

on. Basically, what is needed is that we need to develop a process relationship that uses tools and concepts to ensure information is shared and exchanged; the employee gets it and is able to provide feedback to the boss when and where necessary.

The relationship between boss and subordinate that is grown over time becomes increasingly more important. The best environment is one-on-one interaction, but this isn't always possible. It is absolutely essential for both parties to be able to trust, work together, and, ultimately, communicate effectively.

> One of the best bosses I ever worked for made a point of coming to my work space at least once every week to sit down and talk to me face-to-face about any and every subject I wanted. He used the time to explain what he wanted on particular items he tasked me to perform, but he was sure to make me aware of the fact I was able to ask him any question I wanted on any subject. We were wildly successful on a couple of occasions because I was able to understand what he wanted and, more importantly, why he wanted it. One example that comes to mind was the time the CEO of our large (ten thousand-plus employees) government-owned, contractor-operated facility complained to his direct reports every month for about six months in his staff call that he did not know how much money would be required to satisfy previously existing small contracts that our company had inherited when we won the current contract modification. It worried the CEO because he "didn't know what he didn't know" about what his financial risk might be. Month after month, there would be a major performance review and the CEO would ask if anyone could answer his fairly simple question. Even though my boss wasn't associated with contracts or the financial management of the organization directly, one day, he came to me and tasked me with answering the question. I politely and professionally

whined that since I was so new to the organization, I had absolutely no finance background or experience and no idea where to even begin the attempt to answer the question. My boss directed me to the contracts building and recommended I go there to start. He asked me to just try to find out what was happening and what the risk might be. I did and, after some initial stumbling, finally talked with a contract administrator (literally a little old lady in tennis shoes behind a big stack of folders), who patiently explained in laymen's terms just what had happened and what they were doing to find the boss his answer. Basically, ten years prior, whenever any kind of work had been required on campus in any area from cutting the grass or calling a plumber to fix a toilet, to remodeling a building, a contract administrator would purchase the goods and services needed to accomplish the task. If all went according to plan, the work would be contracted out, performed, and completed and the contract would be closed out. In some cases, though, there would be a modification or a change in design that would require an additional contract, or perhaps the work was not properly performed, or, for whatever the reason, the contract was not completed and therefore not closed out. In order to fix the problem, a group of four individuals were in the process of closing each contract using due diligence by contacting each agency and working out the details. After gathering all this data, I asked how much money we were discussing in rough order of magnitude, if each contract was required to be paid up in full (which was unlikely), and what she thought was a realistic risk amount. The answer came back that, worst case, it could be $5M, but more than likely, it would be less than $100K. I went back to the office, did a five-page PowerPoint slide presentation that defined the situation, what actions were being taken, and the "guestimate" the very patient lady had given me and gave it to my boss. He presented it to the CEO and was highly praised for finally answering the question (note: anytime you can make your boss look good in front of his boss is a good thing). The point is that my boss provided the information and guidance to define what he wanted, and based on our relationship, I was willing to step out on my own and apply his guidance and resources to achieve a recommended goal. His expectations were exceeded because he communicated what he wanted, why he wanted it, and where to go to get it. Also, his confidence in me and my ability to get a simple answer to a relatively simple question made all the difference in the world.

In order to define and manage leadership in our organizations, we must identify goals, recognize where we are, and apply process tools and resources to get to where we want to be.

Leadership Management Goal

The goal of every manager is to lead and guide his subordinates such that they accomplish what he wants them to accomplish. In order to do that, the manager needs to provide his subordinate supervisors with a tool set and process guide to

- assess their performance as supervisors, identify supervisor strengths and weaknesses by group and individual,
- develop and implement supervisor developmental plans to maintain strengths and identify weaknesses so they can be improved and/or mistakes or flaws are eliminated,
- integrate individual performance improvement plans with the annual performance appraisal or review process,
- provide a tool that will identify and begin development of possible future leaders and/or supervisors,
- communicate systemic Issues with recommended solutions to senior management leadership.

Behaviors of a High Performer

- High-performing first-line supervisors are the target audience.
- Developed types of performance necessary to perform tasks at a high level and identifying trends across contract.
- The behaviors list is *not* a comprehensive list of all the tasks first-line supervisors must accomplish to do their jobs but should provide an initial list to start with.
- Result is, "twelve high performer mission essential tasks" with "associated high performance behaviors" highlight those tasks that the interviewees deemed were critical success factors.
- The focus is on the common "high performance" behaviors.

Leader Development Program

The Way we are now:	The Way we want to be:
• No leader development taking place at all.	• Managed and programmed approach to leader development.
• Supervisors win "popularity contest" based on personality rather than capability.	• Manager's become the primary trainers with the correct tools kit to develop leads/supervisors
• Experience based on trial and error rather than planning and execution.	• Managers tailor skill development based on contract requirements.
• Courses are provided based on what's available rather than what's needed.	• Leader skills are focused, aligned, communicated and tracked.
• Unscheduled and unforecasted ad hoc training is the norm.	• Talent management is addressed with each performance appraisal.

Performs Mission-Essential Task Reviews to Establish Leadership Qualities

- What demonstrates leadership in our organization?
- How much understanding of our business processes is required?
- Do our leaders understand how to acquire needed resources?
- How is continuous improvement encouraged and tracked?
- Do our leaders know how to set the conditions to plan for work ahead, understand what it takes to place processes in motion in time to achieve results?
- How well does our organization adapt to change?
- How well does he/she communicate with seniors/peers/subordinates?
- Is he/she technically and tactfully competent?
- Does he/she know where profit comes from?

Demonstrates Leadership

- Displays confidence and competence
- Is responsible and accountable for team's actions
- Understands that confrontation is necessary and acceptable
- Is a self-starter, is proactive, and does not wait to react after the fact
- Acknowledges both praise for good performance and criticism for failure
- Takes action to improve poor performance
- Understands the difference between a risk and a gamble
- Doesn't micromanage subordinates except where necessary
- Does the right thing no matter the circumstance

Technically and Tactfully Proficient Job Skills

- Knows the contract and how the process flows
- Can merge production with quality

- Sets up a network across functional areas to ensure his team does their part
- Understands how best to sequence tasks for best results
- Proactively addresses problem areas
- Understands required technical aspects
- Can visualize his team's performance; doesn't need to be told how well they are performing

Understands Resource Allocation

- Knows how best to access required materials, manpower, and other resources
- Plans ahead for requirements but doesn't waste resources
- Proactively develops solutions and anticipates problem areas
- Knows his/her team; sets the conditions for each to succeed
- Optimizes contacts to ensure he/she has what is needed when it is needed

Seeks Continuous Improvement

- Never stops learning, has personal goals for each member of the team
- Sees continuous improvement as a key part of their daily activity
- Determines why someone fell short (equipment issues, delays, poor skills), then uses feedback to improve the situation.
- Is able to "step back" and ask "why are we doing that?" and develops "out of the box" alternatives.
- Understands that doing a job better is different than just getting the job done
- Is constantly identifying waste and inefficiencies and eliminating them from the process
- Uses feedback as a crew/individual development tool and as a method to flag systemic issues

Plans Work

- Develops daily plan and job assignment (both for self and organization)
- Understands job assignments within work flow
- Forecasts work for employees to match their numbers and skills required
- Controls work flow but "sees" employees to assign them tasks based upon skills and capabilities
- Understands the most valuable asset is time and manages it well.
- Reduces and/or eliminates required but non-value added tasks.
- Has a plan A with several back up plans to ensure productively the entire time.

Communicates Up the Chain

- Is factual (no matter what the ramifications)
- Puts effort in communicating with superiors as well as peers and subordinates
- Is able to translate subjective data (morale, effectiveness) into objective form (meet daily requirements)
- Goes to supervisor with problem and recommended solution (vice "what do we do now?" questions)
- Communicates orally—able to make managers understand
- Communicates in writing—able to compose thoughts
- Communicates with all shareholders (anyone who needs to know about the issue)
- Communicates across stovepipes but works within the chain of command
- Follows up on communications (doesn't just "fire and forget" e-mails)

Communicates to Subordinates

- Listens, uses positive reinforcement
- Ensures all confrontation remains on a professional level (no emotional interference)
- Establishes communication structure (opportunities for feedback)
- Ensures everyone understands priorities
- Maintains presence "on the shop floor" with subordinates

Communicates with Adjacent Managers and Builds Teams

- Develops mutual respect and admiration
- Coordinates "on the same level" with
    - counterparts
    - quality department
    - facilities managers (housekeeping employees)
    - customers
    - suppliers
    - others
- Has a network of subject matter experts (SME) that ensure coordination takes place.

Technically Competent

- Knows the systems, equipment, forms, records, etc., they are working on
- Continuously seeks improvement (knowledge and methodologies)
- Gives clear directions
- Knows where and how to find answers
- Resolves issues at the lowest level possible
- Keeps superiors informed

Develops a Performance-Improvement, Skills-Development Strategy for All

- Based on individual competency (where do you want to be in three to five years from now?)
- Acts within senior leadership authority for approval
- Initiates individual counseling that identifies strengths and weaknesses and how to take specific action to change/improve
- Assigns milestones and apply resources (expect results)
- Makes time each day to communicate, communicate, communicate

Creating a High-Performing Supervisor

- Requires skills, practice, feedback, reinforcement, communication
- Uses tools and checklists, benchmark success, perform "on the job" support discussions
- Writes down unofficial performance appraisals that provide information to the individual
- Spends time with all your direct reports to discuss their performance

Performance Improvement Plan (Example)

General Information
This form documents a plan for required performance improvement (when an employee's performance does not meet minimum expectations).
Employee Name: *John Doe*
Employee Number: *123456*
Classification: *Production Manager*
Department: *Maintenance*

Last Evaluation Date: *24 August 201X*

Job Responsibilities/Priorities

List the employee's primary job responsibilities that require attention and describe the specific improvement that is needed to meet minimum expectations.

1. **Job Responsibility**: Provides leadership to personnel through effective goal setting, delegation, and communication. Aligns goals of the department with the company's goals, policies, and strategies

   Specific Improvements Required: *Isn't well-organized; is easily distracted; needs constant reminders to accomplish essential goals and organizational requirements. Doesn't use a computer or can be relied upon to receive and respond in a timely manner to e-mail traffic.*

2. **Job Responsibility**: Act as a focal point for data pertaining to task accomplishment. Ensures required status reports are submitted in a timely manner.

   Specific Improvements Required: *Requires extensive information technology training and experience. Must often have data printed off in hard copy before he can respond to it. John knows the "big picture" concepts but can't use the tools we have to accomplish the jobs he is assigned. He spends too much time working with other section personnel rather than focusing on his specific job.*

3. **Job Responsibility:** Monitors production workflow to ensure priorities, assignments, and sequences determined in production meetings are followed.

   Specific Improvements Required: *Has a problem setting and keeping priorities; usually signs up for too many tasks and then doesn't follow through. Has a problem accomplishing assigned tasks as required.*

DEFINING AND GUIDING LEADERSHIP

4. **Job Responsibility**: Monitors status, material demand, and satisfaction rates. Should be able to compile and trend data to detect faults/errors and implement appropriate corrective action.

   Specific Improvements Required: *Cannot utilize information technology to perform these and other tasks; requires extensive training and experience using and understanding spreadsheets, the information system, and other available management tools.*

5. **Job Responsibility**: Maintains a working relationship and acts as a liaison with internal and external customers in order to maintain a high level of cooperation and service.

   Specific Improvements Required: *Develop a formal, scheduled working relationship with counterparts and other support members to ensure that all required coordination is accomplished to enhance capability.*

6. **Job Responsibility**: Demonstrates continuous effort to improve operations, decrease cycle time, and streamline work processes.

   Specific Improvements Required: *Requires extensive information technology (IT) training (Microsoft Office, cell phone, Blackberry) and to learn how to use tools provided; requires organizational skill development (setting priorities, following through on actions, and communicating on all levels).*

Behavioral Competencies: Organizational Success . . .
Making People Matter
- Teamwork/Cooperation
- Customer satisfaction
- Commitment to continuous quality / process improvement
- Creativity/innovation

- Flexibility/adaptability to change
- Continuous learning/development
- Displays vision
- Leadership/initiative
- Positive attitude
- Respect for others
- Interpersonal skills
- Supports/understands diversity and related issues
- Honesty/fairness
- Builds trust
- Recognizes others' achievements
- Understands others' perspectives
- Resolves conflicts constructively

Job Effectiveness: Additional Competencies for Administrative Personnel
- Planning/organization
- Problem solving/judgment
- Makes effective decisions
- Takes responsibility
- Achieves results
- Communicates effectively
- Dependability/attendance
- Job/organizational knowledge
- Productivity
- Coaches/counsels/evaluates staff
- Identifies areas and supports employee development
- Opportunities
- Encourages teamwork and group achievement
- Leads change/achieves support of objectives
- Enables and empowers staff
- Strives to achieve diverse staff at all levels
- Understands diversity issues and creates supportive
- Environment for diverse employees

DEFINING AND GUIDING LEADERSHIP

Identify the specific competencies needing improvement from the table above (or any company, department, or job specific competencies previously identified) and describe the performance improvement required.

1. **Competency**: Flexibility/Adaptability to Change
   Specific Improvement Required: *Learn to use information technology tools available to ensure most effective and efficient productivity is achieved. Adapt to new technology techniques provided.*

2. **Competency**: Continuous Learning/Development
   Specific Improvement Required: *Learn to use information technology tools provided to ensure all capabilities are appropriately utilized and all available assets are properly managed, deadlines are met, operational effectiveness is achieved.*

3. **Competency**: Achieves Results
   Specific Improvement Required: *Not only knowledgeable in processes but also able to organize and lead other managers with same or similar tools. Maximizes every opportunity to improve system.*

4. **Competency**: Learn to Use Information Technology
   Specific Improvement Required: *Not only learn to use but embrace new system tools to include a Blackberry phone, time collection, and all other new software improvements.*

5. **Competency**: Planning/Organization
   Specific Improvement Required: *Determine highest priority tasks and separate them from other or "nice to do" items. Focus on performing your job first, then help others.*

Plan Establishment

Support to be Provided by Supervisor (e.g., training, equipment): As we have discussed before, I will make my time available to help you understand how to use the technology tools provided. I will provide additional time and other training resources to you to ensure all your questions are answered.

A Blackberry phone has been requested for you. You must focus on the e-mail system and learn to respond quickly and accurately to same.

The IT directorate and the training section will provide functional experts and training classes as required to assist in your personal and professional development.

Regarding the assignment of tasks and delegation of authority, I will assist you in making decisions and pointing out how to improve in the area of setting and accomplishing priorities.

Plan Establishment Signatures:

Employee:_____Date:_____

Supervisor:_____Date:_____

Director, Human Resources: _____Date:_____

Follow-Up Review

Dates (3) of Follow-Up Discussions:

NOTE: (To be completed within 30, 60, and 90 days of annual review date) The Performance Improvement Plan (PIP) does not eliminate the requirement for the regularly scheduled Performance Appraisal System Evaluation, which must be completed monthly for all administrative personnel.

DEFINING AND GUIDING LEADERSHIP

This review is for the:

☐ 30-day evaluation ☐ 60-day evaluation ☐ 90-day evaluation

☐ Employee has achieved the required improvement described above. Use additional page, if necessary. Comments (improvements must be listed and explained in detail):

☐ Employee has not achieved the required improvement described above. Use additional page, if necessary. The employee has problems in the areas described below (deficiencies must be listed and explained in detail):

Follow-Up Review Signatures:

Employee:_____Date:_____

Supervisor:_____Date:_____

Director, Human Resources: _____Date:_____

After the follow-up review is completed, provide a copy to employee, retain a copy for supervisor's file and send original to human resources office for the employee's personnel file.

Chapter Three

Change Management

Purpose: Describe methodology used to develop the organization's strategic planning and cascade throughout to include individual performance-based management goal setting.

Process: Through a series of conferences and discussions, develop mission statement, vision of future success, communicate contract metrics, and establish process ownership to ensure necessary support is identified.

Objectives: Explain cost (resources required) and time needed

- To ensure focus and alignment to meet contract requirements and customer expectations.
- To provide a framework that establishes a formal process to receive customer guidance, build a plan, and openly discuss vision with country managers.
- To develop a synergistic product for senior leadership that analyzes, integrates, and synchronizes each country's roles and responsibilities.
- To begin process of allocating resources needed for FY08 (ongoing).

CHANGE MANAGEMENT

- To establish a planned starting point of expected performance from which adjustments (audible at the line of scrimmage) can be made as necessary.

Goal: Provide the organization a framework that **f**ocuses on the most important things, **a**ligns resources and assets, **c**ommunicates objectives, set targets in order to **t**rack performance (FACT)

Continuous Process

I. Strategic Focus

Step 1. Refined and commit to strategy

II. Continuous Improvement

Step 7. Track metrics
Step 8. Improvement; revisit goals; cascade

Sustainable Results

II. Assessment

Step 2. Audit measures
Step 3. Develop new measures
Step 4. Apply new measures
Step 5. Analyze & report

III. Change Planning & Implementation

Step 6. Implement Improvement Plans

Organizational change management is the perspective of business leadership from the top looking down into the organization. The emphasis is on communications, training, and the overall culture or value system of the organization.

Individual change management is the management of change from the perspective of the employees. The focus for individual change management is around the tools and techniques to help employees through the transition.

Four Change Management Objectives (that can be achieved using the individual change management approach)

Manage personal transitions. Individuals can assess where they are in the change process and identify their own personal barriers to change.

Focused conversations. Communication with employees can be targeted to where they are in the change process, thereby enabling productive and focused conversations centered on their area of interest or conflict.

Diagnose gaps. Collective input from employees provides a diagnosis of why a change may be failing or is not as effective as planned.

Identify corrective actions. A framework can be created to identify corrective actions during the change process.

The ADKAR Change Management Model

Awareness of the need to change
Desire to participate and support the change
Knowledge, skills, and abilities about how to change
Ability to implement new skills and behaviors
Reinforcement to keep the change in place

ADKAR is a useful tool for focusing conversations about change, diagnosing the root causes of resistance, determining corrective actions, and managing individual transitions.

CHANGE MANAGEMENT

An example of how to manage change happened in my experience when new management assumed control of a repair and maintenance contract for a large organization. The unionized work force had been in place with a collective bargaining agreement that was over 50 years old, and generally held the opinion they were the experts in providing service and maintenance in the industry. Very early in the reorganization phase however, management realized the work force was using outdated safety procedures to perform services particularly in the area of fall protection (the nature of the maintenance effort required the workers to climb in some cases 20 feet off the ground in order to verify that bolts were properly tightened, no damage had occurred, etc). In order to provide adequate fall arrest/protection for the work force the new management determined that both process and equipment utilization had to change. The work force, and even some individuals in lower level management, resisted this effort.

After all, "we have been doing this just fine for all this time," and "who are you to question how we do things?" were comments received on a regular basis. The customer in this situation was briefed, saw the danger, and agreed to an initial trial of two of the new "scaffolding" type fall protection devices. A great deal of money was spent, training was conducted, and the new devices were used. The complaints got worse. Not only was it time consuming to have to reposition the scaffolding devices, the work force generally felt the effort was unnecessary. As the equipment operationally ready rates decreased senior management felt more pressure from both the union and the customer to return to the previous processes. Using the ADKAR methodology described however to make the work force aware, gave them the desire (see the benefits), provided knowledge and skill, and later reinforced and improved processes as we became more used to the equipment), as time went on the complaints came less frequent and efficiency began to increase. Individuals found the scaffolding provided many more capabilities and offered much more freedom of movement than previously allowed which meant a better job could be performed at higher distances. About six months after senior management had been subjected to the worse criticisms by both the Union and the customer, an older woman came to me and thanked me for "keeping the faith" and making the organization use the new fall arrest equipment. She admitted that she using the previous methodology to perform work at great distances off the ground she had been frightened to death and had even suffered injury one time when she had lost her footing and twisted her body to keep from falling.

The whole change process described above took place over a year's timeframe. Senior management knew they were doing the right thing and stood by their beliefs in spite of significant resistance on both sides of the equation (the customer and the work force). Using the ADKAR model and persisting with patience and firm resolve this effort led the way for other change efforts later. The work force (and the customer) came to realize that senior management really did care about their welfare rather than just the "bottom line" profit margin. It was a classic example where doing the right thing paid dividends on all levels and caused the work force to be able to operate in a safe environment throughout the industry culture.

A wise man once told me that in terms of the relationship between the union and senior management that "you get the union you deserve." By that he meant that if you treat the union with disdain and force them to "just do what I say because I'm the boss – like it or not," you will get a work force that tries at every opportunity to resist and revolt to management. If you "treat them like you would want to be treated" with respect and understanding your relationship will be much stronger and more profitable in the long run.

CHANGE MANAGEMENT

In this example, the ADKAR change management model applies as follows:

- **Awareness**: Management spent considerable time and effort explaining why the change was needed including bringing in external agencies who provided fall protection classes, literature, and demonstrations. A heretofore unknown danger was carefully defined and counter measures described in depth.
- **Desire:** By explaining the danger and the new safety requirements that would be used to protect the employees management was able to explain why change was needed. While the set up of scaffolding was initially seen as an unnecessary inconvenience, over time the employees saw it led to improved maintenance capability and that management really did care about their welfare.
- **Knowledge, Skills:** Management spent considerable effort showing the work force how to properly assemble the scaffolding and ensure it was properly used. Within a very short time the employees found quick and easy ways to ensure it was palced into use and then removed.
- **Ability:** Based on the increased capability the scaffolding provided (the employee was no longer having to cling to the ladder with one hand and try to use tools with the other) the ability to perform repair work was greatly enhanced with the new procedures.
- **Reinforcement:** Every senior member of management visited the workplace and provided encouragement at every opportunity. Additionally, monetary compensation (bonus) was provided after the effort was completed. As discussed previously, an effective after-action review not only led to process improvement but also reinforced the belief to each employee they were part of the team and able to positively influence what happened.

Principle—Authority for Change

The number one success factor for implementing change is visible and active executive sponsorship.

Effective sponsorship at the right level may determine success or failure of the project.

Creating an Effective Vision

First draft: The process often starts with an initial statement from a single individual, reflecting both his or her dreams and real marketplace needs.

Role of the guiding coalition: The first draft is always modeled over time by the guiding coalition or an even larger group of people.

Importance of teamwork: The group process never works well without a minimum of effective teamwork.

Time frame: Vision is never created in a single meeting. The activity takes months, sometimes years. Still, it is important to define the general concept for implementation.

End product: The process results in a direction for the future that is desirable, feasible, focused, flexible, and able to be easily explained and conveyed in five minutes or less.

Key Elements in the Effective Communication of Vision

- *Simplicity:* All jargon and "technobabble" must be eliminated.
- *Metaphor, analogy, and example:* A verbal picture is worth a thousand words.

- *Multiple forums:* Big meetings and small, memos and newspapers, formal and informal interaction—all are effective for spreading the word.
- *Repetition:* Ideas sink in deeply only after they have been heard many times.
- *Leadership by example:* Behavior from important people that is inconsistent with the vision overwhelms other forms of communication.
- *Explanation of seeming inconsistencies:* Unaddressed inconsistencies undermine the credibility of all communication.
- *Give-and-take:* Two-way communication is always more powerful than one-way communication.

Empowering People to Effect Change
- Communicate a sensible vision to employees: If employees have a shared sense of purpose, it will be easier to initiate actions to achieve that purpose.
- Make structures compatible with the vision: Unaligned structures block needed action.
- Provide the training employees need: Without the right skills and attitudes, people feel disempowered.
- Align information and personnel systems to the vision: Unaligned systems also block needed action.
- Confront supervisors who undercut needed change: Nothing dampens enthusiasm in people the way a bad or noncaring supervisor can.

Principle—Change Is a Process
- Change is not implemented in a single moment, and likewise, the role of business leaders in managing change should not be reduced to a single event. The manager's role in change must be active and visible in all phases of the change process.

- Success is achieved when a business change is introduced and employees have the awareness and desire to implement the change, the knowledge, and ability to make it happen and reinforcement to keep the change in place.

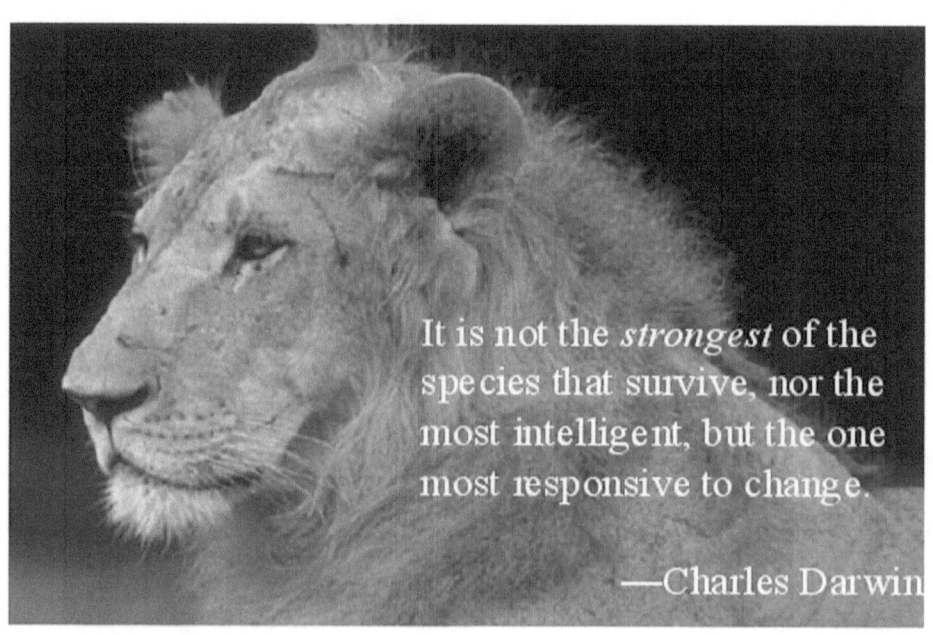

Chapter Four

How to Conduct an Effective Meeting (Working Group Management)

One of the most important issues facing any group or organization is how communication flows from lower levels to/from the decision makers. A continuing process, this action must be managed in order to be effective and have structure and defined roles. In this example, a medium-range company of over one hundred employees needs to have a way of communicating on a regular basis. The working group can be made up of disparate small business units, departments, sections, functional staff section, or directorates. The key is the provision of a set process or procedure each group can use to make contributions to the organization. It's fascinating to see how many large well-developed organizations use poor technique to accomplish this portion of their workday based on the error with a "that's the way we always used to do it" mentality.

Commonly named or referred to as staff call or meeting, there are so many things going on during these gatherings; it is important to develop rules and expectation management if each member is going to be effective not only performing the tasks they are responsible for but also being able to integrate tasks across the organization.

This slide show presentation will provide a general guideline that can be used to develop or improve this part of the organization's communication capability.

HOW TO CONDUCT EFFECTIVE MEETING

★ Working Group Purpose/Function

- Used to address needs and communicate internally and externally across staff sections, including tenants, contractors, higher, lower, and adjacent organizations

- Must be chaired by senior leaders from each organization and stressed by the chain of command

- Maximum use of shared portal will increase efficiency

- Expect constant change—anticipate each group's purpose and function will "morph" over time as the environment and the mission changes

- Each group represented must be prepared to provide input BEFORE the scheduled meeting time

Too many times, members of the group come to meetings expecting to be "fed" rather than accomplishing the meeting's tasks. Actions required to take place before the meeting takes place are as follows:

Before the meeting . . .

- **Define the Purpose and Set Objectives for the Meeting.**
  Before planning the agenda, determine the objective of the meeting. Link to
  - protection, sustainment, enabling civilian authority
  - ensure every section and interested party is represented.

- **Provide an Agenda Beforehand.**
  Distribute the agenda via shared portal (handouts for tenant units) and provide background material so members will be prepared and up-to-date.

- **Assign Meeting Preparation.**
  Use shared portal: give all participants something to prepare for the meeting, and that meeting will take on a new significance to each group member.

- **Assign Action Items.**
  Don't finish any discussion in the meeting without deciding how to act on it (assign responsibility and set response time).

LEADERSHIP MANAGEMENT TOOLBOX

During the meeting . . .

- Start on time, end on time, stay on strategic level.

- Review the agenda and set priorities for the meeting.

- Stick to the agenda (stay out of the weeds).
  Encourage group discussion to get all points of view and ideas.
  Encourage feedback, ideas, activities, and commitment to the organization.

- Assign tasks, set time lines, demand commitment, and results.

- Keep minutes of the meeting for future reference.

- Summarize assignments reached and end the meeting on time.

- Set a date, time, and place for the next meeting.

Most importantly, make the meeting mean something. Take notes and publish them for those missing or for future reference.

After the meeting . . .

Write up and distribute minutes within three days.

Follow up on delegation decisions. See that all members understand and carry out their responsibilities.

Objectives should be SMART:
Specific
    Measurable
        Achievable
            Realistic
                Timely

Put unfinished business on the agenda for the next meeting.

HOW TO CONDUCT EFFECTIVE MEETING

Ensure Mission/Vision/Purpose

- What are our primary goals?
- How do we support our employees?
- Are we effectively communicating our processes?
- Provide refuge from the storm
    - Protect integrity
    - Sustain the process
    - Understand, Visualize, Describe, Act

An uninterested observer is required to evaluate the effectiveness of the process from time to time to avoid complacency and maintain focus. This slide provides metrics to be considered. The questions to be answered during the P6T3SFI analysis help to make sure all aspects are considered.

Analysis Tools

P6T3SFI

P6	T3	S	F	I
Problem:	Time:	Safety:	Facilities:	IT:
Plan:	Tools:			
Priorities:	Training:			
People:				
Parts:				
Publications:				

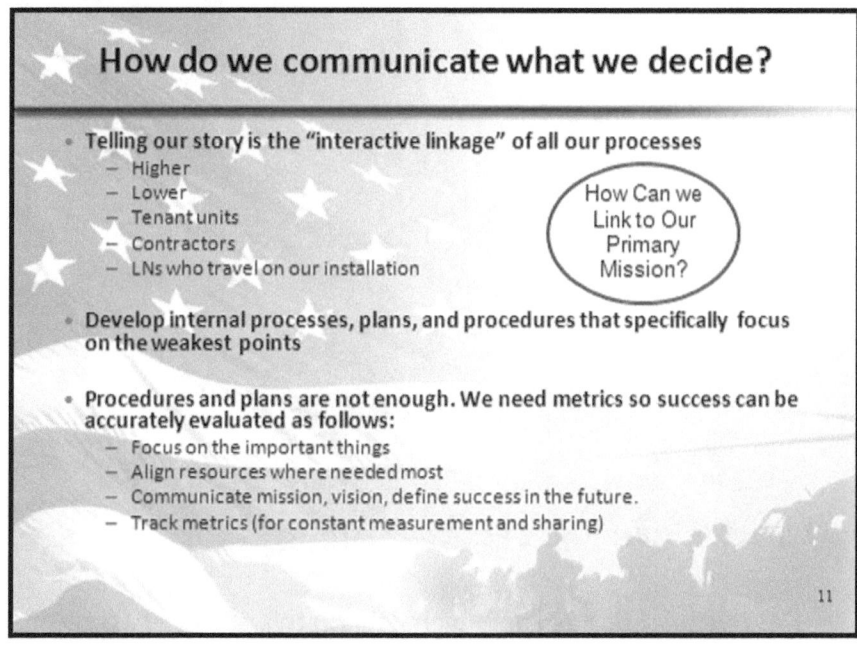

This slide defines each level's role in the process.

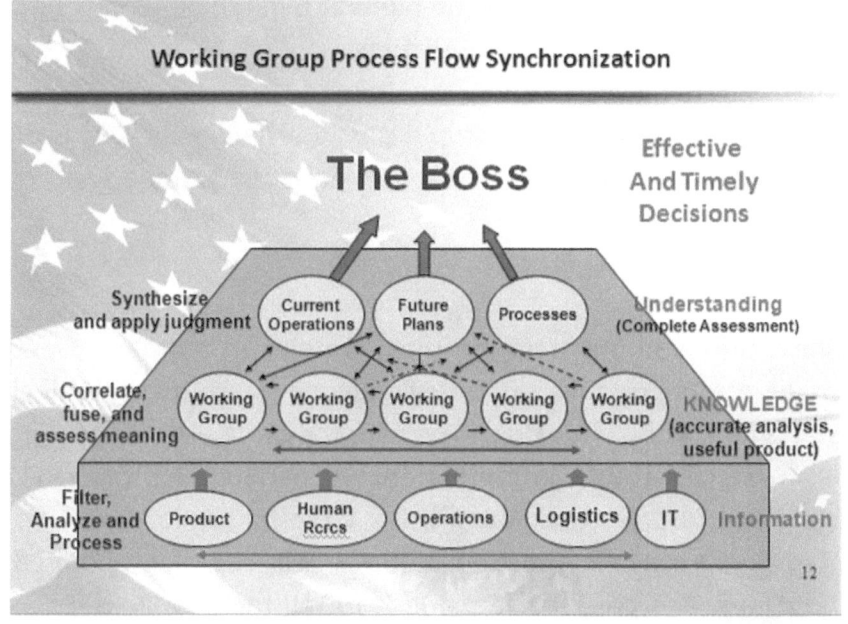

Chapter Five

Parlor Tricks

How Smart Is Your Right Foot?

- Try this out; a lot of brain cells were lost on this. It takes two seconds.
- Without anyone watching you and while sitting at your desk in front of your computer, lift your right foot off the floor and make clockwise circles.
- Now while doing this, draw the number 6 in the air with your right hand. Your foot will change direction.
- There's nothing you can do about it.
- You and I both know how stupid it is, but before the day is done, you are going to try it again, if you've not already done so.

Close Eyes, Point to North

The next time you are trying to make a point to a group of people regarding the importance of strategic planning, ask them to all close their eyes and, without looking, to point to the cardinal direction—north (or east, west, or south, your preference). Then instruct them to keep pointing and to open their eyes. If it's a typical group, some will be pointed in the correct direction, but you will see many pointed on all directions. The point to be made is to tell them while the correct direction is this way, the point is not so much which way is correct as much as making the point that through communication and by working together as a group; we need to all point in generally the same way. Our senior leadership will steer us in the correct direction, and our task is to all work together to get there.

Myers Briggs and Other Personality Performance Assessments

There are several types of personality assessment tools available for review. While they are interesting and have the potential for providing leadership techniques and enhanced understanding of individuals, it must be stressed that all activities associated with this information is worthless unless tools are provided that will cause the information to be used in some form of realistic fashion. Another way of expressing it would be to say that unless the personality performance assessment is accompanied by a series of discussions and with a set of tools to explain why it is important and how best to employ the information gleaned from the assessment, it serves no useful purpose.

In one organization, I was pleased to see one particular section manager using the personality factors each of her subordinates had to a useful purpose. After tasking them with learning about what it was and completing the personality testing (online at no cost), she actually used the results to help the individual work on their problem areas. In short, if the person was introverted, she encouraged them to recognize this factor and try to become more outgoing; to her judgmental employees, she encouraged them to use their gut feeling more, etc. She not only grouped opposites together for group projects, she also encouraged them individually and counseled them during the annual performance appraisals.

Communication Happens despite Our Spelling

The Google search engine feature (among others) has replaced our need for memory cells to remember who scored that winning touchdown in the 1978 Orange Bowl. In the chaos of being able to communicate over several different mediums, using several different means a separate language came into existence. A kind of unauthorized shorthand was adopted that allowed individuals to send and receive messages almost in code. Taking advantage of a relatively unheard of capability we have for cognitive recognition to understand written words even when the letters are placed out of correct sequence (see below), communication happens.

Cna yuo raed tihs?
fi yuo cna raed tihs, yuo hvae a sgtrane mnid too
Cna yuo raed tihs? Olny 55 plepoe out of 100 can.
i cdnuolt blveiee taht I cluod aulaclty uesdnatnrd waht I was rdanieg. The phaonmneal pweor of the hmuan mnid, aoccdrnig to a rscheearch at Cmabrigde Uinervtisy, it dseno't mtaetr in waht oerdr the ltteres in a wrod are, the olny iproamtnt tihng is taht the frsit and lsat ltteer be in the rghit pclae. The rset can be a taotl mses and you can sitll raed it whotuit a pboerlm. Tihs is bcuseae the huamn mnid deos not raed ervey lteter by istlef, but the wrod as a wlohe. Azanmig huh? yaeh and I awlyas tghuhot slpeling was ipmorantt!

Chapter Six

Balanced Scorecard, Lean/Sixth Sigma, and Other Process Improvement Activities

What Is a Balanced Scorecard?

Balanced scorecard is the process that uses FACT (*focus* on the most important things to satisfy our customer, *align* everyone's job so that each individual is most effective at performing critical tasks, *communicate* our plan for the future to our customers and our employees, and *track* performance to ensure we are using resources adequately). Basically, it not only answers the question whether or not we are properly balanced doing the right things and doing things right.

Organizations use the balanced scorecard to monitor performance, plan for the future, and allocate resources to ensure customer satisfaction. It is a continuing improvement process and is incorporated into every aspect of planning process development.

Balanced scorecard can also be the major focus of individual performance-based management process. It is applicable at all levels of the organization and ensures that all business units are focused and well-aligned with objectives that ensure overall success. It involves a "cascading" of guidance while ensuring upward feedback, cross-organization synchronization and integration and incorporates a strong customer focus.

The author (center) with Balanced Scorecard creators, Norton and Kaplan, at a book signing event at a BSC Conference in San Diego, 2006.

At the foundation is a focus on continuous process improvement. Each manager is charged with identifying potential improvements for the processes and systems he/she employs and manages. The expectation is that managers and supervisors at every level, within every organizational element, and every employee to proactively seek continuous process improvement.

Benefits of a Balanced Scorecard

Why should the balanced scorecard approach be used?

Focus:
- The balanced scorecard zeros in on what is most important and lays out the priorities.
- Every worker knows what is expected of him or her and how they can contribute to the future success of the business.

LEADERSHIP MANAGEMENT TOOLBOX

Alignment:
- Balanced scorecard creates alignment of short-term action with company strategy.
- Strategy becomes the central organizational agenda for all employees at all levels.

Communication: Balanced scorecard causes each member of the organization to communicate and share understanding of the most important things that need to be accomplished in order to satisfy the customer.

Tracking: Each objective is selected and metrics established with ownership chosen so that the contract can be accomplished and verified once it is completed.

Using the balanced scorecard is like "open book" management; leadership shares this information with all employees in the form of targeted goals and measures. With this common knowledge, leadership allows all employees to contribute to the company's strategy and communicate strategic vision, resource allocation, and performance status.

Mission: What the organization is about; the purpose, intent, and vision of success (needs to be succinctly stated and easy to remember). One example may be *"We fix automobiles so you can drive them safely for a long time."*

Vision: What we want to accomplish in the future; our dream or a picture of what success looks like in the future. An example might be *"We will protect and develop our employees so we can win future contracts."*

Company Core Values: This is a statement of guiding principles; what we believe in—the ideals, principles, and philosophy at the center of the organization. Examples might be as follows:

- *Integrity (always tell the truth whether our customer wants to hear it or not)*
- *Safety (protect our employees no matter what it costs)*
- *Quality (we should strive to do it right the first time)*
- *Customer focus (ensure we win the contract every day)*
- *Taking care of people (more than safety, treat others as we would like to be treated)*

Customers:
Who is the direct beneficiary of our services or products?

Strategic Themes:
Main focus areas of the business; used to focus staff effort on accomplishing the vision.

Strategic Results:
Desired outcomes for the strategic themes.

Strategic Objective:
Continuous improvement activity that must be done (what we are going to do).

Strategic Initiative:
Action programs designed to achieve our strategic results (how we are going to do it).

Strategy Map:
Cause-effect relationships among the objectives. The strategy map helps tell the story of how initiatives are to be accomplished.

Perspectives: Different views of our organization. Defines what "lenses" we should use in order to describe our strategy (organizational readiness, internal processes and growth, customer, financial).

Strategy: How we intend to accomplish our vision; an approach or game plan.

Sample Standard Operational Procedure Guide

PURPOSE: To provide guidance at all levels of leadership on balanced scorecard development for their area of responsibility.

OBJECTIVES:
- To establish the balanced scorecard programs and procedures to ensure alignment of each unit's business strategies, objectives, and initiatives with senior leaders and with the overarching values, goals, and strategic planning.
- To ensure that business objectives and performance measures are integrated and supportive across organizational boundaries. Each unit must work with their internal and external customers to develop goals that, when achieved, will result in mutual success.
- To keep senior leadership fully informed of any changes in process requirements that may affect operations.
- To guide and train management in the formulation of balanced scorecard management systems and tools designed to meet stated objectives.

RESPONSIBILITIES:

The *chief executive officer* will initiate the BSC cycle and will approve each level's organizational goals.

Senior managers monitor the overall operation of the BSC cycle through daily/weekly contact with management, process owners, BSC committees, coordinators, and the workforce.

The *program manager*, BSC (as designated), will provide oversight and planning for all BSC off-site conferences to include concept approval, preparation, and on-site performance (with assistance as necessary from other directorates).

BALANCED SCORECARD

The BSC coordinators monitor major activities to assist, guide, record progress, and then communicate successes throughout the contract. Each sub-element will have an assigned BSC coordinator who will focus on the actions, activities, and progress for each field/activity.

The *program manager*, BSC, is responsible for tracking the success of objectives by keeping statistics, defining initiatives, and recording progress.

PROCEDURES:

Development of a balanced scorecard is the first part of the performance management process (Fig. 1). It is crucial because it sets the stage for ensuring understanding and commitment to what it must do to ensure overall organizational success. Balanced scorecard goal setting ensures each business unit focuses some quality time on establishing performance objectives, metrics, targets, and initiatives to guide the organization's major activities for the following term.

PERFORMANCE MANAGEMENT PROCESS

Sub-Process	Balanced Scorecard development	Progress Reviews	Midyear Performance Review	Progress Reviews	Final Performance Review
Outcome	Scorecards	Updated scorecard	Discussion on performance, formal feedback, and development plan	Updated scorecard	Discussion on performance, formal feedback, and development plan
Time frame	1st Quarter	Quarterly, monthly, or weekly as desired	3rd Quarter	Quarterly, monthly, or weekly as desired	2nd Quarter (following FY)

Feedback, Counseling, Midcourse Adjustments as Appropriate

Goal setting and alignment for balanced scorecard development must be accomplished by leaders at every level in the organization and consists of the following steps:

> **Step 1: Assessment.** Gather information and conduct mission analysis to determine specified and implied tasks.
> **Step 2: Strategy.** Determine business strategy that will be required to accomplish mission tasks.
> **Step 3: Objectives.** Convert tasks into specific objectives.
> **Step 4: Strategy Map.** Map out the cause-effect relationship for each objective. Assign responsibilities for each objective.
> **Step 5: Performance Measures.** Develop a balance of metrics that measure strategic and operational progress, leading and lagging indicators, with target levels of performance.
> **Step 6: Initiatives.** Determine the initiatives and "tactics" needed to accomplish the objectives at the target level of performance. Define supporting requirements.

Some of these steps can be done concurrently at various levels of the organization. For example, all levels may concurrently begin gathering information and conducting mission analysis. However, some of the steps will need to "flow down" from higher levels of leadership to middle management to team supervisors. For example, senior leadership guidance on key areas of focus, improvement expectations, or accountability for special projects will need to be articulated and may cascade into objectives and initiatives that affect multiple levels of leadership.

The Six Steps for Balanced Scorecard Development

Step 1: Assessment

To determine annual goals and objectives and correctly align them with the organization's vision, each leader must have a solid understanding of how their unit contributes to the achievement of those objectives. While they may already have a good understanding, well-performed goal setting and alignment calls for careful *analysis* of the *organization's intent*. (It helps if you think of the unit as one of the "rowers" responsible for moving the corporate "boat" rapidly along its course to the finish line.) While the leaders may begin this mission analysis alone, it is normally wiser to get key members of their team involved to assist in gathering relevant information and interpreting it in order to more fully understand and define the unit's goals and objectives.

Information needed to effectively perform vision analysis is likely to come from several sources. The figure below lists many relevant sources that would be useful in defining your organization's vision:

Key Documents	*Contractual Requirements*	*Other Guidance/ Feedback*
Strategic Plan	**Contract Specification**	**Customer Comments**
Annual Operating Budget	**Requirements**	**Supplier Feedback**
Supplemental Goals Priorities	**Schedules**	**Self Assessments**
Policies and Procedures	*Reports*	**Supervisor Guidance**
Core Values	**Audits**	**Surveys/Focus Groups**
Labor Resource Plan	**Safety Rates**	
Capital Plan	**Financial Reports**	
	Performance Data	

Sources of Information for Mission Analysis

The table above is not comprehensive in scope. Other information not listed might be relevant for any given organization. It is the leader's job to ensure adequate information is reviewed to fully understand what each sub-element will have to do to fulfill or exceed their part in success. Some of the corporate-level documents may not be available to first or second echelon supervisors, but it is important that sufficient guidance "flows down" from higher-level areas to allow these frontline leaders to perform successful mission analysis and develop objectives and initiatives that support the larger organization's goals.

If any leader doubts that they have adequate information to perform this piece of the process, they should ask their supervisor for clarification. As a rule of thumb, each leader should not only understand the mission of the business unit they lead but also that of the next higher organization and the next higher (two levels up), at a minimum. Thus, it would behoove them to gather the right information to understand these missions clearly.

Beyond gathering hard information, the leader should also explicitly solicit guidance at this stage from their supervisor and from their customers. What priorities do they see as important for the unit in the coming year? What measures of success will they be looking for?

Once the information is gathered, the leader and his team are ready for the assessment phase. The team will include direct reports, but the leader may want the help of other key or high-potential subordinates. While some leaders may wish to do at least part of the work by themselves, a participative process will be more robust and will more likely result in collaborative and integrated approaches. In any event, the leader's direct reports need to understand one another's obligations to support major goals that require cross-departmental or cross-divisional support, and including them is a great way to create or deepen this understanding.

Organizational Assessment Analysis, put simply, is the process of analyzing plans, guidance, documents, performance metrics, feedback and other relevant information, and "facilitating" which tasks that the unit must accomplish for the coming year to successfully "row its oar." These tasks can be either specified or implied.

Specified tasks are relatively easy to identify. They are clearly spelled out or stated, and often well-defined. For example, a specific production line must produce 150 items a day to maintain scheduled delivery of product. *Implied tasks* are not specifically or clearly stated anywhere. Instead, they are "implied" because to achieve a stated objective (such as a key financial target), certain things must be successfully accomplished even if they are not explicitly mentioned in a plan, report, or other guidance. An example of an implied task could be the provision of adjustment of staffing levels to support a requirement to reduce man-hours. Obviously, once an *implied* task is identified, it can be translated into one or more *specified* tasks for lower-level business units.

The key to performing an organization assessment analysis is understanding what your unit can and must do to contribute optimally to the overall success of the organization. In doing so, you must think in terms of end-to-end processes, inputs and outputs and understand the interactions of units that feed one another as a supply chain and give the strongest consideration to both your internal or external customers. Thus, up-front activities like recruitment and hiring must have goals that feed the success of follow-on activities.

The outcome of mission analysis is a list of specified and implied tasks that the leader and his team then use to develop strategies and concrete objectives for the coming project term. The complete list should include tasks related to performance, to employee and leadership development, and to advancing the values of the company within the leader's subelement. The importance of explicitly listing the tasks derived from mission analysis and communicating them among the leader's team cannot be overstated as this is the real beginning of alignment.

Step 2: Developing Strategies to Accomplish the Mission

> *The essence of strategy is in the activities, choosing to perform activities differently, or to perform different activities than rivals.*
>
> —Michael Porter, Harvard University

The purpose is to develop a list of strategic themes or categories that define the overarching strategic approach. For example:

- **Operational Excellence:** Optimize use of resources in a safe environment while continuously improving the quality of our product.
- **Employee Commitment:** Become a high-performance, team-based learning organization.
- **Customer Retention:** Expand business opportunities by exceeding our customer's expectations.

Within this framework, each business unit will determine its unique strategy to support overall success. By reviewing performance data and organizing the list of tasks developed during step 1 by strategic theme, each business unit can clarify its game plan and focus on the areas that will have the most impact.

Begin by grouping the tasks developed in step 1 under strategic themes. Each task from step 1 is then examined and placed in the appropriate corporate thematic area. The goal is to group like tasks that support the strategic themes. Once the tasks are grouped under the appropriate themes, each task is examined with a goal of developing an objective based on the tasks. Essentially, the themes used in this example—operational excellence, employee commitment, and customer retention—are defined with specific tasks assigned in order to achieve each theme. The outcome of step 2 are clearly defined actions and activities supporting each of the strategic themes, which are defined, resourced, communicated throughout the workforce. Additionally, each area is tracked to ensure completion and, where necessary, resources are applied.

Step 3: Converting Tasks into Objectives

To ensure clarity of expectations, eliminate confusion as to what defines success, and to facilitate progress measurement throughout, the tasks identified in mission analysis are converted into measurable objectives which are SMART (**s**pecific, **m**easurable, **a**ttainable, **r**ealist, and **t**imely).

Objectives should be both challenging and clear. They are the continuous improvement goals of strategy. Objectives need to communicate the action people must undertake to implement strategy. As the basic building blocks of strategy, they are the business drivers that, when related to one another, form a cause-effect linkage between the work that is performed and the desired results to be accomplished.

For each strategic theme, the key objectives that describe the theme are defined and business unit strategies are resourced and managed. When developing objectives, it is important to use action verbs combined with a noun for objective statements (e.g., implement a new process, improve cross-training of employees, enhance access to information systems, etc.). Then associate each objective with a perspective and assign individual performance goals.

Step 4: Strategy Mapping

For each strategic theme, link the objectives in cause-effect relationships. Write each objective in a short-action-oriented phrase and draw an oval around each one. Draw a line between related objectives and indicate the logic flow (if-then) with an arrowhead showing the "cause" pointing to the "effect." Start at the top with the "effect" and work downward through the "causes" to show all the potential causes for a desired "effect" or result. Test your logic by working from the bottom to the top (e.g., "*If* I improve the skills mix, *then* cycle time will be reduced.").

You will find that some objectives won't fit into a cause-effect relationship, either because they are themselves initiatives or projects or they are not strategic objectives. You will also find that some "causes" or "effects" are missing. You should then revisit your strategy and identify additional objectives or relationships.

Figure 3, 4, and 5 show example strategy maps.

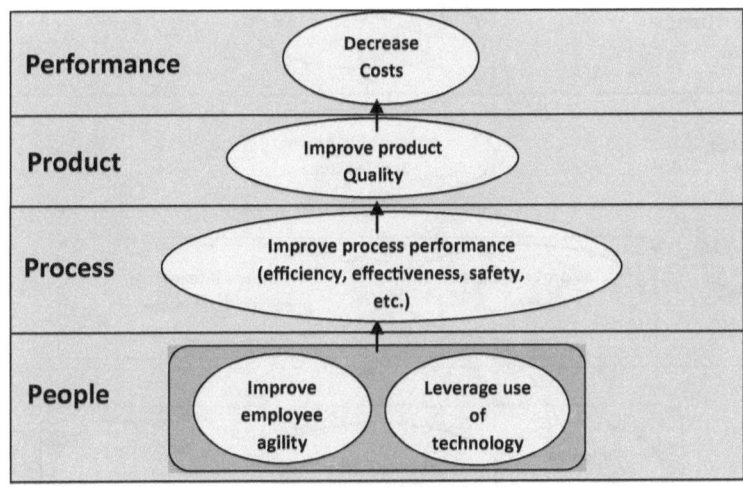

Figure 3

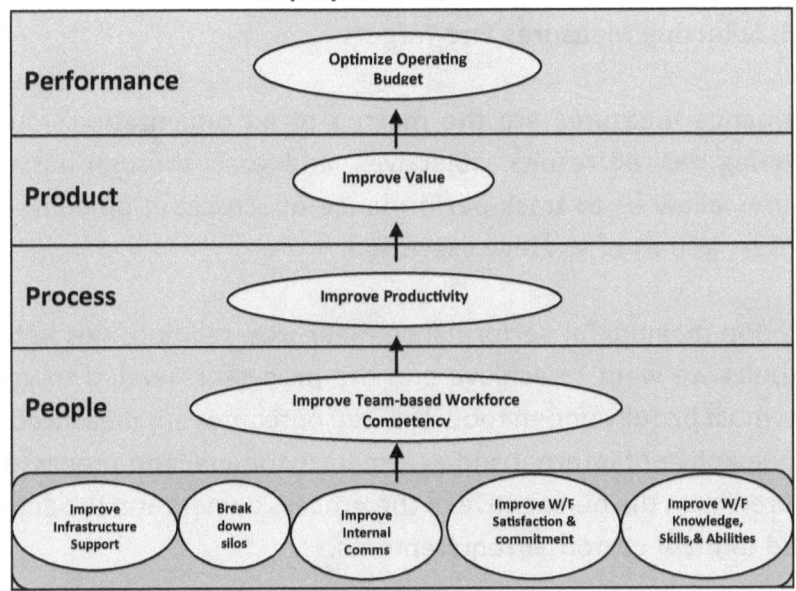

Figure 4

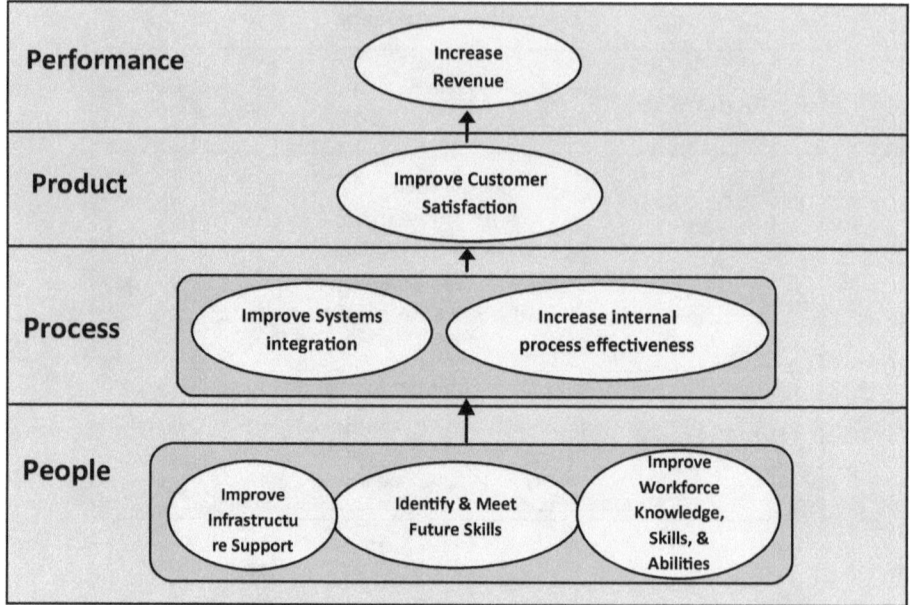

Figure 5

Step 5: Selecting Measures and Targets

Performance measures are the metrics of an organization's success in meeting desired results, objectives, and goals through initiatives. Measures allow us to track performance of scorecard objectives and initiatives, as part of strategy execution.

To develop meaningful performance measures, relationships between the results we want to achieve and the processes needed to get the results must be fully understood. Desired outcomes are measured from the perspective of internal and external customers, and processes are measured from the perspective of the process owners and the activities needed to meet customer requirements.

> There are two categories of performance measures:
>
> <u>Lagging</u> measures are indicators of past performance that show how successful we were at achieving our goals. Lagging indicators are typically financial and include output (what is produced) and outcome (what is accomplished).
>
> <u>Leading</u> measures are indicators of performance that are precursors of future success. They are the performance drivers that typically measure input (resources consumed) and process (transformation system).

For each strategic theme and its objectives, list the measures and targets that are crucial to accomplishing the desired results. It is important to include at least one measure for each objective.

Step 6: Prioritizing and Selecting Initiatives

Initiatives are the projects and activities used to test strategic hypothesis and drive strategic performance. Initiatives can be discretionary investment projects that encompass one or more objectives.

List the initiatives that should be considered to help meet the strategic objectives. Next, list the criteria that you will use to evaluate and rank the proposed initiatives to determine the final set of selected, prioritized initiatives, programs, and projects. Assign weights (in percentages) to each of the criteria so that the weights total 100 percent. Figure 6 is an example of ranking criteria with assigned weights.

BALANCED SCORECARD

RANKING CRITERIA	WEIGHT
Strategic Importance	40%
Cost	25%
Time to Implement	15%
Complexity	20%
Total	100%

Figure 6

Then on a matrix, assign scores from 1 to 10 for each initiative for each of the criteria. In the example criteria, for strategic importance, a high score would be used for the greatest values. For cost, time to implement, and complexity, a high score would be used for low value. For example, a very low cost initiative would receive a score of 10. In this way, the initiatives that will return the most in the shortest time with the least cost would be ranked highest.

Multiply each score by the weight percentage for that criterion and place that number in the matrix to the right of the score. Then add the weighted scores to get the weighted totals for each initiative. Rank them with 1 being the highest priority. The outcome of step 6 is a prioritized list of proposed initiatives.

Figure 7 is an example of an Initiative Prioritization Matrix.

INITIATIVE	RANKING CRITERIA SCORES I TIMES WEIGHT				WEIGHTED TOTAL	RANK
	Strategic Importance	Cost	Time to Implement	Complexity		
	I	I	I	I		
	I	I	I	I		
	I	I	I	I		
	I	I	I	I		
	I	I	I	I		

Figure 7

LEADERSHIP MANAGEMENT TOOLBOX

Formalizing Focus Area/Initiative Checklist—to Remove All Misunderstanding and Assign Responsibility and Accountability

Element	Description
Project Name	
Process Owner Who is responsible for this initiative?	
Process Leader	
Team Participants Who is best suited to provide needed input and expertise for this initiative? Workers, suppliers, customers, facilitators	
Project Statement In simple terms, what is the issue to be addressed? What is the gap between expected and actual performance? Be specific: who, what, where, when, and how often?	
Project Scope What are the limits and scope of this initiative? What is not included? Be specific: who what, where, when does it include/exclude?	
Goals and Standards What are the time limits; how will success be measured? Address job performance, metrics, baselines, and goals?	
Impact What is expected to be the resulting output? How will it enhance customer value? State benefits and detractors.	
Time line—Milestones Provide an anticipated time line. Define success and completion—prevent scope creep in any form.	

BALANCED SCORECARD

Resources Required/Assumptions and Risks:

Corrective Action Plan
Customer Focus Areas

On the Shop Floor:	With Customer:
• Initiate Communication • Verify need/expectation • Separate customer • "How to" Training req'd	• Centralize communication • Verify desires in writing • Offer assistance with Staff Actions • Make successful • Follow up
With Contracting Officer: • Need closer relationship • Regularly scheduled structure • Interface with Customer	**With Corporate HQ:** • Find ways to assist • Customer has shown interest in hearing from Senior Executives • Can correlate with Contracting Rep • "How to" Training req'd

- Senior Staff Personnel not conversant in customer viewpoint;
- "We-they" mentality abounds

How do we Start the process?

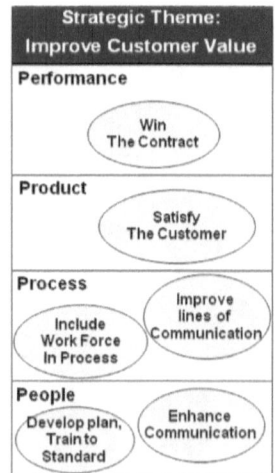

Strategic Theme:
Improve Customer value

	Objectives:	Measures:	Targets:	Initiatives:
	Actions needed to achieve strategy (game plan)	How success in achieving the strategy will be measured and tracked	The desired level of performance	Key action programs required to achieve objectives

Objectives	Measures	Targets	Initiatives
Improve Customer Perception Of value	Type and frequency of Interaction (3 levels)	Per Time Schedule	Develop Newsletter; Inform Work Force

Management is the integration of separate processes and the application of resources to a project or activity to achieve a set goal or objective. Whether conducting a symphony orchestra, playing a football game, or making coffee, various amounts of training may be required; a process applied in order to produce a product or service. And if more than one event is desired, it is possible for the performance of the process or product developed to be analyzed and compared for efficiency and possible improvement. While there are many methodologies available to study management theory and application, the concept of analyzing activities from four perspectives—people, processes, product, and performance in order to manage activities, communicate vision, and predict future success—is a concept called balance scorecard. Developed at the Harvard Business School in the early '90s by Dr. David Norton and Robert Kaplan, balanced scorecard is the name given to a strategic planning and management system that links activities to the organization's vision and strategy for achieving goals and objectives of the organization. It also incorporates internal and external communication and allows for the development of a shared common operating picture that can be used to monitor performance. Many of us have observed and personally experiencing the management of processes and application of resources over time; beginning in its simplest forms by observing how members of a family interrelate, then continuing through early childhood and participating in various interactive societal programs, we learn how processes work. We develop rules and routines that seem to work best in our circumstance. Many are well versed in management practice and the understanding of how the application of change management, resource allocation, and process improvement tools impact groups of people formed together as groups or organizations. In discussions relating to process improvement, the development of and continued use of process analysis through Lean concepts is another level of awareness and can lead to fascinating discoveries. Using what I will call group think and other common sense tools, you can very rapidly increase efficiency and manage asset distribution such that virtually all waste is eliminated. The study and application of management theory, including project management and the Lean/Six Sigma processes, are valuable to any industry, the concepts useful to all facets of process improvement.

For example, some time ago, I developed pain in both my left and right thumbs that required surgery. Because of the physical therapy that would be required following the operation, the doctor performing the treatment recommended doing the left thumb first and then the right thumb several weeks later; so that is what we did. The operations were a complete success, and I was very pleased with the results. I mention this because the processes that were used for the two operations that were performed by the same doctor, in the same hospital, and with the very same nursing crew for the same malady, same time frame (within three months) were completely different from one another. The location and application of the intravenous needle, anesthesia, length of time in recovery room, paperwork completed after versus before the procedure, and other items were not even remotely similar in nature. During one of the follow-up visits, I mentioned the disparity to the doctor and expressed how surprised I was there wasn't more standardized uniformity. He admitted that it was a problem the hospital was working on and one they had discovered ultimately leads to mistakes, rework, and wasted time. I told him how Lean concepts could help him identify and eliminate waste in his processes. He was amazed that process analysis used in the aviation repair, maintenance, and overhaul industry could equally apply to the field of medicine.

The next time you visit a McDonald's restaurant, take notice of the processes used to receive your order, process, and deliver the food by way of the drive-through window. Using a speaker phone and well-established processes, young inexperienced minimum wage workers are able to understand your order, process it and prepare your food, receive payment, and provide what you ordered (food) to you with nearly the same standard as inside the building at the restaurant counter. In my experience, it seems the customer outside going through the drive-through have priority over the customers inside standing face-to-face with the clerks. The standardization of processes performed by nonskilled, inexperienced workers is masterful in concept and execution. Beginning with the standardized packages of

LEADERSHIP MANAGEMENT TOOLBOX

food (number 3 is a quarter pounder with cheese meal, order of fries, name the drink), the quickness of the order is further enhanced by the "read back" capability of the intercom monitor (showing you what you ordered, what it costs, how it will be served) and ushers you to the next window where you pay (as the clerk is simultaneously placing the next order to the customer behind you). From there, you drive to the next window where your food is being handed to you (and you can usually see what the person two places behind you has ordered because it is being prepared also). Inside, a similar dance is taking place with each food type being prepared, including the french fries, hamburgers, milk shakes, apple pies. Although I haven't counted, I believe the menu holds about twenty items to choose from. When was the last time you noticed an error in this process? Yes, it does happen, but it's rare. You hear about people being burned by coffee that's too hot and possibly getting the wrong order or receiving the incorrect burger, but it's the exception rather the rule and hasn't happened to me in probably the last two hundred times I've gone through the drive-through. How is this possible with a rotating workforce that is paid minimum wage but is the very reason for its financial success? McDonald's is a leader in process management.

Another example that comes to mind is a company that specializes in the maintenance, repair, and overhaul refurbishment actions for late-model machines. As our economy continues to evolve, it has been determined that it is cheaper to overhaul an older machine rather than buy a new one. Almost immediately, a whole new industry sprang to life based on the refurbishment of aging machines. The basic concept is to receive an older piece of equipment that is thirty-five to forty-five years old, tear it apart, fix or replace all the components, and then rebuild it so that it can be utilized good as new again. Although wildly successful initially, recently this organization developed a series of problems in their work flow that ultimately led to delayed delivery dates and several quality performance issues. Upon investigation, it was determined the processes they use to conduct this activity had been modified as part of a restructuring activity. Unfortunately, this company had increased the amount of work coming into the shop without adding facilities or adjusting the processes used to perform the work. In the time it took to increase their ability to handle the additional workload, the reputation they previously enjoyed with their customers was severely damaged. Their product suffered due to inappropriate and out-of-date process management.

These examples are process management issues that influence day-to-day activities. It doesn't make any difference if you are baking cookies or sending folks to the moon; the effective management of processes and application of resources will define success or failure. When the doctor realized he has a standardization problem for his patients, it might be appropriate for him to look to the solutions that McDonald's has provided to improve his standardization. No one at the repair/refurbishment facility intentionally failed to adjust their processes to accommodate the increased workload; they simply were not able to identify and implement effective process change. The magic in process management is understanding the relationship between people (organizational readiness, training, facilities, human resource development, etc.), process (internal process management improvement or how to actually apply resources in order to get things completed), product (customer focus on products and services), and performance (financial prosperity—more money coming in than going out), and how each perspective impacts successful accomplishment of organizational goals and objectives.

One of the key responsibilities for any manager is to analyze trends and identify all possible areas for improvement. The key is not just being responsible for providing all aspects of asset utilization and integration but also seizing the opportunity to improve all processes and procedures. The use of concepts explained in Kaplan's and Norton's balanced scorecard methodology provide the tools needed to see and make adjustments through change management, improved communication, and a multitude of process improvement opportunities, which ultimately result in cost savings.

During the balanced scorecard certification classes and conferences I attended (where I managed the balanced scorecard for an organization composed of seven separate business units within an aviation maintenance service contract), the main questions being asked by individuals representing organizations that were just beginning the balanced scorecard process were, "How do you start? What is the process to begin the effort? How do I go from ideas to action?" By attempting to link balanced scorecard concepts to process management, many of these questions are answered. There are other important pieces and parts to be incorporated also, but my primary effort will be to link concept to action, fundamental idea to tool, and perspective to management process.

Whether you are changing a diaper, building an automobile, or painting a picture, you will need some amount of training, will use a process, provide a product (hopefully), and perform the task to some degree of favorable conclusion. The integration of processes and application of resources requires management methodologies to accomplish established goals and objectives. By incorporating the four primary balanced scorecard perspectives into process improvement activities such as Lean/Six Sigma and other activities, I believe any industry can improve their ability to provide products and services, reduce costs, and enhance customer satisfaction.

Balanced Scorecard: Unit Assessment, Analysis, Communication, and Synchronization Tool

Situation Description:
Over the recent years, there has been unprecedented change in our nation's use of technology—socially, economically, and in the work environment. Some of these changes placed us in new territory and

resulted in a different way to look at how we are doing business. The requirement to outsource more and more tasks and functions traditionally performed by in-house employees resulted in the need to incorporate a better way of communicating and working with desperate groups and develop relationships with this additional resource (let's refer to the newly defined role of outsourced resources as the contract civilian work force—CCWF). While not clearly identified, defined, or understood (depending on the type product or service being provided), the situation has developed where the CCWF is depended upon to perform the bulk of the organization's administrative, compensation, maintenance, construction, and other major efforts. At the same time, when the utilization of outsourcing is increasing, less and less information is made available to address how to properly utilize this asset. While some effort has been spent detailing how the contract will be monitored and administered, there is no forum established to capture the organization's vision and best practices or to communicate clearly discernable goals or metrics for success. What is missing is a system or procedure to assist in the interaction between the controlling organization and the outsourced contractor.

Both groups need to be synchronized and aligned in terms of defining value and establishing what success looks like. Action needs to take place early in the relationship that causes each side to analyze requirements and incorporate coordinated planning actions so as to not only effect mission accomplishment but satisfy the customer hopes, wishes, and desires (HWD) as well. Discussions are required where the controlling organization explains goals in a joint planning cycle that produces a workable plan. This not only makes for a better plan, it also ensures a common operating picture for all concerned.

Customer satisfaction (see definition of "above and beyond" requirements versus "stated contract requirements" later in this article) happens when effective communication takes place, and both parties share a vision of what right looks like. In this discussion, we will talk about what rules of engagement must be addressed as well as methods to achieve continuous process improvement. Oftentimes, the valued CCWF resource is depended on to be at least as capable, resourceful, efficient, and proficient as employees in the controlling organization would be; in the technical fields, more so. How does one learn to manage this asset? What procedures are in place to help the one express what is needed to enhance mission performance? Who makes the determination whether the organization's readiness is red, amber, or green in a particular area or predict what it will be in the future? What is the process to allocate resources? In the business world, these and other questions can be addressed by the use of a planning tool called the balanced scorecard. The use of the balanced scorecard can and should be used as part of the normal annual planning cycle particularly in those situations where a CCWF is planned.

Solution

> *People and their managers are working so hard to be sure things are done right, that they hardly have time to decide if they are doing the right things.*
> —Stephen R. Covey, author,
> *The 7 Habits of Highly Effective People*

The balanced scorecard is a *strategic management system* for establishing and communicating your organization's mission, vision, and strategy to every member of the organization and for aligning each of those aspects. It is simultaneously a multidimensional way of analyzing our processes and a strategic management system and provides a vehicle framework for organizational communication.

Within a balanced scorecard, you will coordinate and align day-to-day operations and process work with your annual strategy. The balanced scorecard, as viewed from different perspectives of organizational performance, provides a framework for planning and measuring strategy. After establishing key areas, metrics, and targets, the BSC tracks and measures success and guides the selection of strategic initiatives.

BALANCED SCORECARD

Balancing Act: Operational versus Strategic Focus

The balanced scorecard management tool allows you to use a process to examine what your primary requirements are and determine ways to achieve them. Similar to Lean concepts, this communication process must be top-down driven from the senior leadership. This isn't a piece of software you can purchase and it will "do it all for you." The key to success is the communication process that we go through determining what it is we do, what task we are to perform, and how best, we as a group, should proceed. We use tools to prioritize our efforts, make assumptions, glean specified and implied requirements, and communicate planning. The charts below illustrate making the business case and defining how to allocate resources to achieve a specific goal.

The next step is to assign objectives, measure, baseline (very similar to task, condition, standard) and establish a way we are to get there. Another way to look at the process is to use the following steps:

Step 1: Assessment. The senior leader meets with his/her management staff and discusses requirement issues including those tasks deemed to be the essential task elements that include what it is the organization is going to provide and to what standard. Determining the organization's strengths and weaknesses, opportunities to improve, and what threats exist that could jeopardize task completion are critical discussion points. This discussion is referred to as analyzing our pains, commonly referred to as weaknesses and threats, and enablers, called opportunities and strengths. See the SWOT chart below:

This shared experience is vital to team building and commitment buy-in for all concerned. No matter how experienced or familiar each member of the group feels he/she is, there is always something learned and "aha" moments that are valuable to the communication process. If performed correctly, each side moves from a "we/they" relationship vantage point to an "us" and "our" unit mentality. This is vital to effective communication and effectiveness.

SWOT Analysis

Strengths	Weaknesses
• What advantages do you have? • What do you do well? • What relevant resources do you have access to? • What do other people see as your strengths? In looking at your strengths, think about them in relation to your competitors - for example, if all your competitors provide high quality products, then a high quality production process is not a strength in the market, it is a necessity.	• What could you improve? • What do you do badly? • What should you avoid? Consider this from an internal and external basis: Do other people seem to perceive weaknesses that you do not see? Are your competitors doing any better than you? It is best to be realistic now, and face any unpleasant truths as soon as possible.
Opportunities	Threats
• Where are the good opportunities facing you? • What are the interesting trends you are aware of? Useful opportunities can come from such things as: • Changes in government policy related to your field • Changes in social patterns, population profiles, lifestyle changes, etc. • Local Events A useful approach to looking at opportunities is to look at your strengths and ask yourself whether these open up any opportunities. Alternatively, look at your weaknesses and ask yourself whether you could open up opportunities by eliminating them.	• What obstacles do you face? • What is your competition doing? • Are the required specifications for your job, products or services changing? • Is changing technology threatening your position? • Do you have bad debt or cash-flow problems? Could any of your weaknesses seriously threaten your business? Carrying out this analysis will often be illuminating - both in terms of pointing out what needs to be done, and in putting problems into perspective.

Step 2: Strategy. Good organizations perform routine tasks routinely. How do we expect to accomplish our mission? How do we take the processes we have developed and accomplish what we need to do? By analyzing the process from each of four perspectives, the picture

becomes clearer. The questions asked on the following chart focus the discussion:

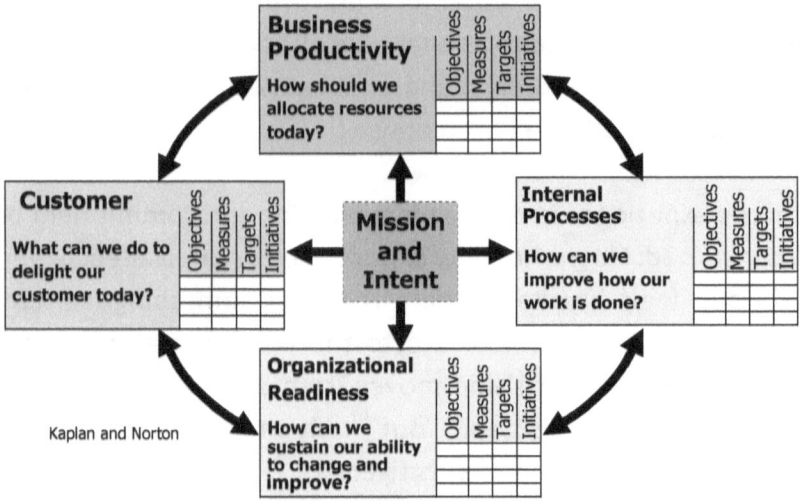

Step 3: Objectives. Convert specified and implied tasks into specific objectives and assign ownership, responsibility, and measurable, attainable metrics. Define success. What does right look like?

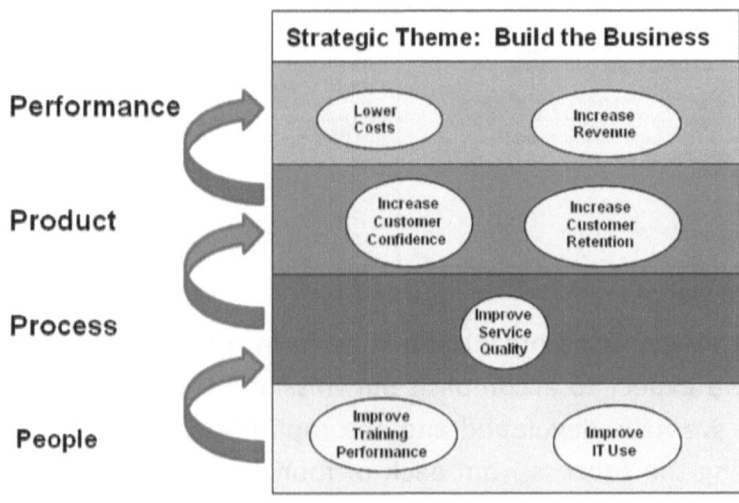

Step 4: Strategy Map. Map out the cause-effect relationship for each objective. Assign responsibilities for each objective.

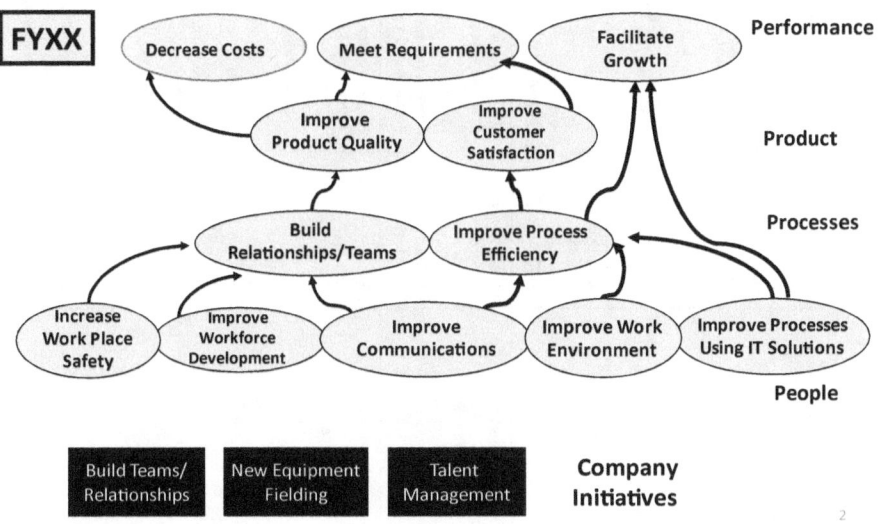

Strategy Map Example

Step 5: Performance Measures. Develop a balance of metrics that measure strategic and operational progress, leading and lagging indicators, with target levels of performance. Measures include the following:

- Performance metrics define success in achieving desired results
- Should be quantifiable
- Should communicate behavior that is required such as
  - Customer satisfaction/retention
  - Quality assessment/evaluation program
  - Employee development (individual and collective)
  - Timeliness of products/services delivery
  - Productivity—process efficiency
  - Compliance
  - Cost

BALANCED SCORECARD

Step 6: Initiatives. Determine the initiatives and tactics needed to accomplish the objectives at the target level of performance. Define supporting requirements.

Strategy Map with Objectives, Metrics, Targets, and Initiatives

Strategic Theme: Operational Excellence	Objective Definition	Metrics	Targets	Initiatives
Business Productivity	-Decrease Cost	-Manpower -Lost Time Rate -Overtime -REJECT Rate	-Reduce % -TBD -Reduce by 5% (Previous Year) -Days	-Disciplined Process Control -Review Staffing
	-Maximize Profit	-Mission Performance -Daily Process Rate	->98% ->80%	-Improve QA ratings - Introduce ISO 9001
Customer	-Meet Customer Requirements -Improve Quality	-Contract Launch Reqmnts -Maint. Non-deliv. -1ST Pass Yield -FMEA	-Meet 100% -92%/85% <7.5%/2% -TBD	-Wal-Mart Greeter -Develop Checklists -Spot Check daily -Improve Tie-in
Internal Process	-Improve Efficiency and Productivity -Lean/Sixth Sigma	-Preventive Maintenance -Benchmarking -Best Business Practices -Configuration Control	-3 Man Hours <1,200 Man Hours -80 Man Hours -Reduce by TBD -2/5 Days	-Phased approach -Tracking Board -Spot Check -Cheat Sheet (Known Problem Areas) -Production Standards
Organizational Readiness	-Improve Communication	-Incidents of Tie-in Commo Breakdowns -Current Status Updates -Self-assessment	-Reduce	-Electronic Status Board -Supervisor/Lead -Commo Initiative -TV Safety Tips -Promote Safety
	-Increase Safety Awareness	-Property Damage	- Reoccurring Incidents	
	-Improve Time Management	-Timeliness of Reports -Effective PC Meetings -Report Internal Target Date	-Reduce Previous Year by 50%	-Time Management Coaching -KeyReport Tracking System
	-Improve Proficiency Through Training	-Establishment of Training Plan -Accomplishment of Planned Tng	-100% -100%	-Training Plan -Maintenance Mentoring System
	-Maximize IT Solutions	-Needs Identified	-100% -80%	-Cost Point Training -Automated Status -Phased procurement

Strategy Map (diagram):
- Business Productivity: Decrease Costs, Meet Requirements, Growth
- Customer: Improve Product Quality, Improve Customer Satisfaction
- Internal Process: Improve Process Efficiency, Build Relationships/Teams
- Organizational Readiness: Improve Communications, Improve Processes Using IT Solutions, Improve Work Environment, Improve Workforce Development, Increase Work Place Safety

How to improve performance: Linking Individual Performance to Corporate Performance

The employee performance evaluation system should be managed and reflect achievement based on goal achievement. In an effort to achieve continued success and employee performance, employees and their supervisors work jointly to establish individual goals that not only enhance Company performance, but also nourish and encourage individual development. Establishing individual goals that are tied to corporate goals and objectives are the responsibility of the employee's immediate supervisor. These goals must be clearly stated with measurable and clearly identified achievement.

The most important factor in this process is Communication. Employees must know what is expected of them by their supervisors, and that their progress and accomplishments are being properly evaluated. The framework of performance improvement is making sure the employees understand how their actions impact the Corporate processes.

Developing Performance Measures

Measures:
- Are performance metrics of a business' relative success in achieving desired results, objectives, and operational goals
- Should be quantifiable whenever possible
- Communicate the behavior that is required to achieve objectives

    1. Customer Satisfaction/Retention
    2. Quality
    3. Employee Development
    4. Timeliness of Services
    5. Productivity – process efficiency
    6. Compliance
    7. Cost

BALANCED SCORECARD

How do you improve Performance?

By improving the Product.

How do you improve the Product?

By improving your processes.

How do you improve the Processes of your organization?

By improving Organizational Readiness.

How do you enhance organizational readiness (People)?

By enhaning training, facilities, communication, information technology, recruiting, hiring, counselling, etc.

Strategy is a hypothesis based on cause and effect relationships, defined by drivers which will create desired outcomes.

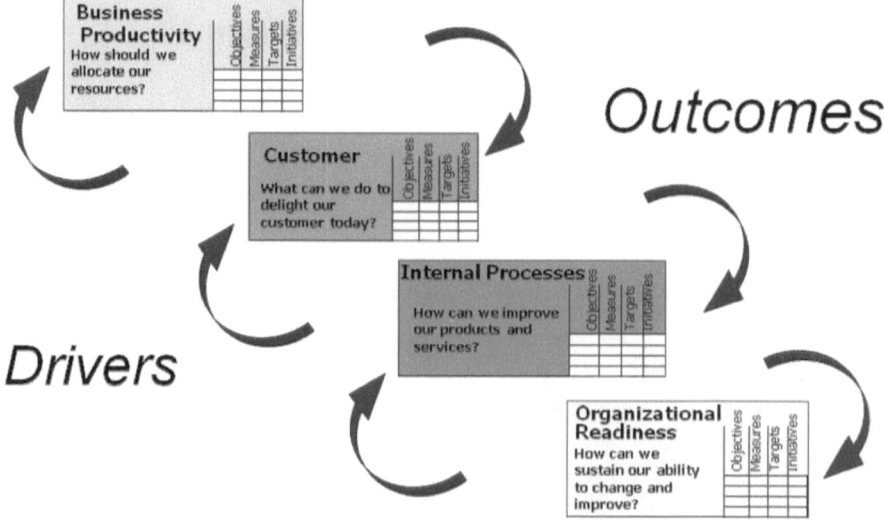

The cause and effect of these drivers result in improved performance over time.

Cause and Effect Hypothesis

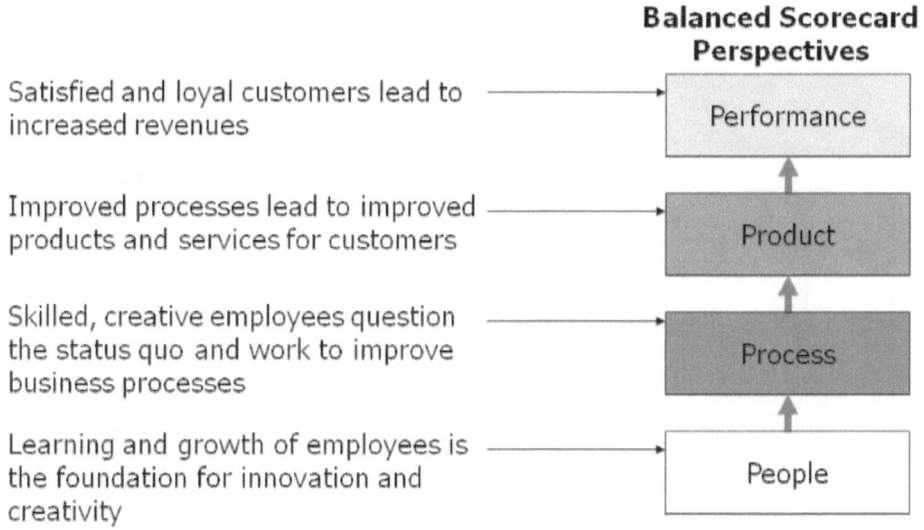

Equally important is the establishment of what is required to exceed expectations. There must also be a process established that identifies and assists those who need improvement in some facet of performance that does not meet expectations.

Understanding the standard deviation of any group of employees allows management to measure organizational readiness and provides the degree of training (and ultimately, resource allocation) in any given situation. Employees scoring in the lower 15% should be placed on a Performance Improvement Plan (PIP) to help increase their work performance to an acceptable level within a 90-day period.

A bell curve is a graph used to illustrate the standard deviation. An example is below.

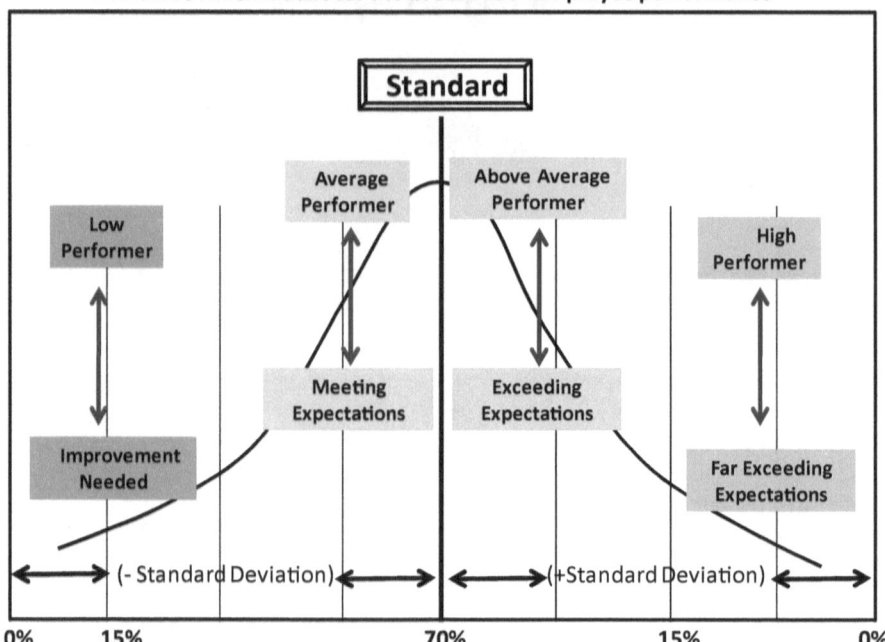

Bell Curve which illustrates the breakout of employee performance

Common Rater Errors

Common errors that are made when rating subordinates are as follows:

- Halo Effect: Rating an employee higher than is realistically possible. The individual is expected to start off as average, and then by performance considered either above average is any particular area.
- Central Tendency: Providing a rating of average or around the midpoint for all qualities.
- Strict Rating: Rating the individual consistently lower than the normal, overly harsh in rating performance qualities.
- Lenient Rating: Rating consistently higher than the expected norm; being inconsistent in determining quality based of other

than job performance factors (this is the most frequent error made by untrained and/or unmonitored raters).
- Latest Behavior: Rating influenced by the most recent behavior; failing to recognize the most commonly demonstrated actions during the entire rating period.
- Initial Impression: Rating based on first impressions; failing to recognize the most consistently demonstrated behaviors during the entire rating period.
- Spillover Effect: Allowing past performance appraisal ratings to unjustly influence current ratings.
- Status Effect: Overrating employees in higher-level jobs or jobs held in high esteem and under-scoring employees in lower-level jobs.
- Same as Me: Giving the rated employee a rating higher than deserved because the person has qualities or characteristics similar to those of the rater.
- Different from Me: Giving the rated employee a rating lower than deserved because the person has qualities or characteristics dissimilar to those of the rater.
- Performance similarity rating: Two or more dimensions on a performance instrument follow or closely relate to a similar quality.
- Contrast Effect: Rating an employee against the performance of another recently rated employee.

To minimize these types of errors, supervisors should keep notes and provide evaluations on a regular basis; also it's best to rate the entire group, put it aside for a while and then review placement of individuals in relation to the group.

Performance Measures

Objective:

Measures	Type	Units of Measure	Measure Owner	Collection Frequency	Baseline	Target	Benchmark against

Chapter Seven

How to Conduct an Adequate After-Action Review

No matter what industry you may find yourself, there are special events that take place from time to time that require special handling. Whether they are recurring events, like parents' day at your elementary school or the production cycle for a special order, when out of the ordinary events take place, management should conduct a review both in process and following the event to learn from and improve the process. This review process is called an after-action review (AAR). It is a structured review process that allows leaders and individual participants within organizations to discover for themselves what happened during the event under discussion, why it happened, and how they can possibly perform better in the future. The purpose of the AAR is twofold. First, it allows everyone to discover for themselves what happened during the event and why. Secondly, it allows the organization to learn from itself so that the organization, as a whole, can improve future performance.

The AAR is a professional discussion that leaders conduct after each major event; the discussion focuses directly on how the process lead to task accomplishment. It stresses meeting standards and is not emotional or a fault-finding investigation; it does not determine winners or losers.

The AAR involves individuals and leaders in the analysis of preparation, coordination, and action and brings out and reinforces important learning points. It's absolutely critical to the process of learning and improving project process. Additionally, if used frequently, it becomes a valuable tool that not only improves the specific task at hand but also tends to leave each participant more aware of his/her responsibilities as each new event occurs while assessing accountability. In anticipation of future AAR discussions, individuals remember and act accordingly during subsequent activities knowing that it might be a discussion point for the group later.

Parts of an AAR

There are four parts to an AAR:

1. There is a factual review of what actions (planning, coordination, directing, controlling) should have happened.
2. A factual statement of what actually happened (disregarding why or who is at fault).
3. Determine what went right or wrong (usually by identifying the three most significant good things that happened and three process failures).
4. Determine how it would have been better to perform the task differently should there be a next time.

AAR Action Process (How to Conduct/Lead the Discussion)

- Set the conditions: To begin the discussion, the leader should gather everyone who participated in the event in a single room. There should be a large chalkboard (or equivalent device) that is used to record (and allow everyone to see the results as they are developed) each discussion point (aids in learning).

HOW TO CONDUCT AN ADEQUATE AFTER-ACTION REVIEW

- Discuss what should have taken place: Everyone who participated then reviews the overall plan that explains what should have happened (or what was originally intended) during the event; many times, this is surprising to some or all the participants.
- Discuss what actually happened: The leader next identifies as objectively as possible what did happen and when (include external agency input, viewpoint, and actions).
- Things to be sustained: What three things should be retained for the next time—what went well or what was successful during the event. (The list can include more than three items, but if more than five items are addressed, you should consider breaking up the subject into smaller areas. For example, divide the action up into preparation, conduct of the event, and then follow-on actions to prevent too detailed a discussion.)
- Things that require change: This is when the leader must be careful and not allow the AAR turn into merely a critique session. If possible, assign ownership for each area to be improved. For those areas that no one is responsible for (for example, perhaps the weather was bad or the problem is too large for the small group to address), consider placing the item into a "parking lot" to be discussed later.
- Determine the approved solution: Finally, as a group, determine how the task or mission should be performed differently the next time you receive a similar tasking. A critical role in guiding the AAR discussion is that the conclusions reached must be SMART (specific, measurable, attainable, realistic, and timely) so that the group can decide exactly how to perform differently the next time.
- When and Where: You should plan AARs to take place during the process and then at the completion of each phase or turning point. AARs provide immediate feedback and reinforce and increase the learning that takes place as a result of the event itself.

AAR Versus Critique

It is important to remember that an AAR is not a critique. A critique has only one viewpoint, usually that of the senior management or leader. This does not allow for individual observations, discussion of events, and learning from others' comments. Critiques are less effective than AARs in getting the most from everyone's experience. Moreover, the limited and often biased point of view of a critique prevents the open discussion of the event. A critique also prevents people from learning from their mistakes. AARs are not critiques because they do not determine success or failure. When you use an AAR, you avoid lecturing your employees in what went wrong, and this makes it better and easier for them to learn.

Types of AARs

Now that we've seen the difference between an AAR and a critique, let's discuss the types of AARs which leaders may conduct. There are two types of AARs: formal and informal.

Formal: The formal AAR is resource-intensive and requires more detailed planning, coordination, preparation, and resources. Organizations normally conduct formal AARs at the senior management level. Leaders normally schedule and conduct formal AARs as a part of external and internal evaluations. At the close, the AAR leader summarizes comments from the observers, covering the strengths and weaknesses discussed during the AAR. This summary also covers what needs to be done to correct major weaknesses.

Informal: The AAR that you will participate in most of the time will be the informal AAR. Smaller organizations usually conduct informal AARs for small groups (three to five) individuals assigned to a crew or when resources are not available to conduct a formal review. Informal

HOW TO CONDUCT AN ADEQUATE AFTER-ACTION REVIEW

AARs require less preparation and are often on-the-spot reviews of performance. These AARs are important since they involve all leaders in the participating organization. Leaders can have discussion comments recorded to use in follow-on AARs or can immediately apply the lessons learned as the process is repeated. The actual conduct of the two types of AARs is very similar.

Chapter Eight

How to Develop and Implement Corrective Action Plan Your Customer Will Accept

Corrective Action Planning Concept

Purpose: Provide information on concept of operations and planned actions to be taken to correct deficiencies found on product delivery item. Included in this effort will be a discussion about how this organization will incorporate change management, reorganize assets, increase frequency of external system evaluations, institute internal and external training to address shortcomings, and enhance the processes used to perform inspections. Specifically, to restore confidence in this organization's ability to properly correct deficiencies noted, improve processes and procedures, and maintain resources, management needs to demonstrate corrective actions to meet customer expectations.

HOW TO DEVELOP AND IMPLEMENT CORRECTIVE ACTION PLAN

Corrective Action Plan-Name
Agenda:

- Change management
- Reorganize assets to maximize readiness (people, process, product, performance)
- Where we are (lack of training and presence)
- Near-term actions
- Estimated completion dates
- Timeline
- Training initiatives
- Additional actions taken
- Summary

Change Management: Using a process that manages organizational change, this organization will increase awareness of the need to change through more frequent external inspections, restore confidence, incorporate training and knowledge development to enhance abilities, and establish reinforcing training programs to ensure lasting results. Taking lessons learned from the previous successful programs, management will carry the change-management process across the contract for use at all other locations.

LEADERSHIP MANAGEMENT TOOLBOX

Corrective Action Plan - Name
Change Management Process

ADKAR

- **Awareness:**
  - Increase inspection influence, frequency of inspection, and presence on shop floor
  - Develop inspection checklists for specific problem areas—preservation of components (even a caveman could do it)
- **Desire:**
  - Personnel change-out—manager
  - Discussion with support from on-the-ground employees
  - Discussion with support from customer
- **Knowledge:**
  - Internal and external training required
  - Verification/validation of process at every step
- **Abilities:**
  - Increase level of understanding and comprehension/communication between management, customer, and workforce
- **Reinforcement:**
  - Initiate certification program

Other: Enhance processes and procedures with more extensive/effective checklists

Where We Were: This organization has identified problem areas and will reorganize assets from other areas to bring relief as quickly as possible. Beginning with organizational readiness, processes will be improved and enhanced to restore confidence in the integrity of the products and services being delivered on-site. By partnering with the employees, management will research the source of current problems (site specific faults found), incorporate prevention technologies, and share technology improvement concepts and corrective actions at this site and across the contract.

HOW TO DEVELOP AND IMPLEMENT CORRECTIVE ACTION PLAN

Corrective Action Plan - Name
Where we were

Disturbing Problem Areas:
1. State facts relating to improper actions
2. Detail what was wrong without excuse or explanation
3. Identify and eliminate improper procedures at every station

Process Change: Increased Presence:
- Insert verification process for each area and along each step
- Increased use of checklists—perform "by the book" processes
- Enhance/increase levels of communication to ensure understanding at every level

Process Improvement: Training:
- Internal and external
- Use industry benchmarking to validate standard
- Eliminate unauthorized and unsupervised action

Time Line: By actually depicting a time line, all shareholders can more easily visualize what steps need to take place and the schedule for when it will happen.

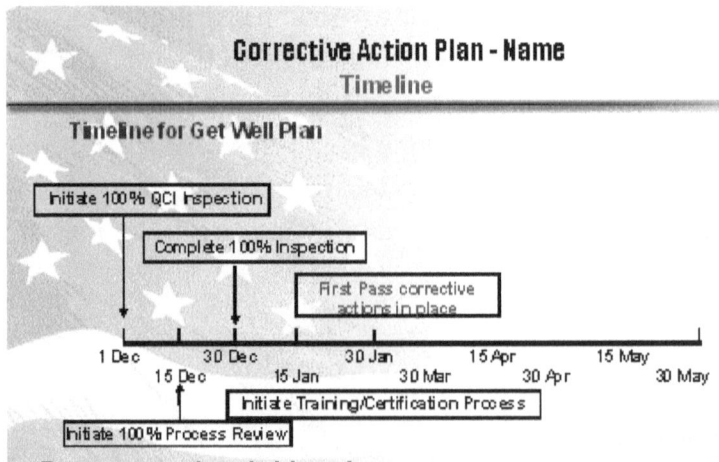

- Process review initiated
- State other factors that may impact recovery process (hiring qualified personnel, movement to work site, etc.
- Set reasonable time line—realistically manage shareholder expectations

LEADERSHIP MANAGEMENT TOOLBOX

Near-Term Actions: The first step is the first step. These are actions probably already taken but need to be recorded.

Corrective Action Plan - Name
Near Term Actions:

- Initiate and record communication processes
- Establish a reporting format and structure (each day/week/month) that is appropriate for your contract
- Initiate training process improvement
- Meet with workforce (calm nerves and explain path forward)
- Increase training frequency and output
- Meet with all shareholders to ensure understanding and need for change
- Increase management presence ASAP (possible use of temporary-hire personnel to assist)
- Address senior-level management personnel actions

Manage Expectations by Providing Realistic Estimate to Classify actions in terms of near-, middle-, and long-term goals and define success.

Corrective Action Plan - Name
Manage Expectations by Defining Success:

Specific
Measurable
Attainable
Realistic
Timely

- Near-Term: Define immediate SMART goals taken and successes achieved
- Mid-Term: Set intermediate goals even if these will require to be changed eventually
- Long-Term: Once Corrective Action Plan is completed, express long term benefits and goals.
- Sustainment Initiatives: Include application of resources at timely intervals

Training Initiatives: Many opportunities to improve should present themselves once the spotlight is shown on the faulty area. The point to remember is that an active quality assurance program will establish fault according to the following list of root causes and descriptions:

Root Cause List and Description

Human Factors: Lack of teamwork, lack of communication, lack of assertiveness, lack of knowledge, lack of resources, lack of awareness, fatigue, stress, distraction, pressure, negative norms, and complacency.

Erroneous/Inadequate Work Instructions: Documents used in the aircraft maintenance program, which includes but not limited to aircraft maintenance manuals, IPCs, SRMs, etc., that are incomplete, vague, misleading, or missing.

Erroneous/Inadequate Data Entry/Documentation: Documentation/records that are erroneous/inadequate, which is limited to any kind of typographical errors, transposed numbers/letters/processes followed but wrong information entered during process.

Insufficient Resources: Resources not available to properly accomplish assigned tasks, which include but are not limited to tooling, ground equipment, fixtures, and manpower.

Faulty Equipment: Equipment failure thru design or performance causing the inability to complete the task properly, which includes but is not limited to tooling, ground equipment, and fixtures.

Erroneous/Inadequate Policies/Procedures/Processes/Contracts: This would include policies/procedures/processes/contracts that are documented in publications and company regulations. This would also include any policies/procedures/processes/contracts that are found to be missing including missing/inadequate interfaces.

Not adhering to Work Instructions/Policies/ Processes/Procedures: Policies, procedures, or processes that are not followed as documented in publications, company regulations, and any manual used in aircraft maintenance.

Inadequate Training/Qualification/Skill: Individuals not trained or qualified and do not possess the skill level necessary to complete the assigned task.

Inadequate Facilities / Work Environment: Conditions that include but are not limited to such things as poor lighting, ventilation, noise, and access to the airplane that would have a direct impact on the quality of work.

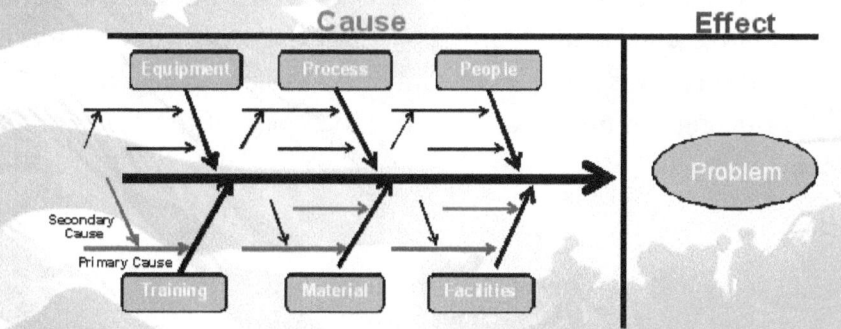

HOW TO DEVELOP AND IMPLEMENT CORRECTIVE ACTION PLAN

Additional Actions Taken: In addition to communication and application of resources for increased training/awareness, other actions may be necessary.

Corrective Action Plan - Name
Additional Actions Taken

- Increased Management presence on the floor, and increased training/Awareness on:
  - Following proper procedures: "by the book"
  - Preservation of process control and fault prevention
- Revitalize/enhance employee development process with newly developed training
- Increase hands-on training and oversight (use of temporary hire personnel)
- Review additional clerk/administrative resources (to allow more effective use of resources time on shop floor)
- Increase productive man-hours (increased training and certification process required)
- Restore confidence in process control of program

Change management is required in processes and procedures to effect meaningful improvement that will get results and last. Training and adherence to "by the book" process compliance and procedural driven activity will enhance organizational readiness. Two things are needed to cause change and restore confidence in the eyes of your customer. The first is direct, personnel involvement by senior management. The second is making the effort to listen to the "voice of the customer" a continuing process.

SUMMARY CONCLUSION

This discussion has been an attempt to provide a one source document that identifies those processes and procedures that are most effective in exploiting the most underutilized and mismanaged resource available to us, our employees. What I have tried to provide in this document is a grouping of tools that should be used to manage leadership in organizations. I did not invent or create these tools and have tried very hard to acknowledge the original creators or authors of these recommended tools like Balanced Scorecard and Change Management. What I have attempted to do is show you which tools I think are best and how best to use them in order to communicate, direct, control and manage your work force.

The ancient warrior from China, Sun Tzu, was a military general and philosopher who lived over 2400 years ago in China fighting battles with bows and arrows. He wrote *The Art of War* based on his experiences, providing strategic principles that are still in use today. He provided timeless wisdom that focused on ends (goals, strategic focus) rather than means (what tools we use to reach our goals). His influence still Inspires soldiers as well as politicians today and is applicable in today's business environment. Sun Tzu dealt with the effective/efficient use of scarce resources, demanded the planned management of resources and implemented leadership management in its purest sense:

SUMMARY CONCLUSION

- *"Do not repeat the tactics which have gained you one victory, but let your methods be regulated by the infinite variety of circumstances."*
- *"By taking into account the favorable factors, he (project manager) makes his plan feasible; by taking into account the unfavorable he may resolve the difficulties."*
- *"Know your enemy and know yourself, your victory will not stand in doubt."*

I know the tools discussed in this book work because I have tried them and found them to be the most effective way to focus, align, communicate and track performance. Whether you are providing a product or service, running a State or local government, managing health care for a hospital, providing administration for a school system, or setting up a small business selling cup cakes these tools will make your job easier and more effective. Most importantly though, they will allow you to harvest your most valuable and important resource, your employee talent and capabilities.

Beginning with communication, this most important capability should be managed so that the concepts senior management wants to transmit is specifically formulated to address the most important concepts. There is a famous rumor (that has not been verified by any official source) about a conversation that took place between then President Kennedy and a janitor at Cape Canaveral during the early stages of the race to the moon. As the story goes, President Kennedy was touring the facility and came into a room where a janitor was mopping the floor in a white suit with mask, gloves, booties on his shoes (complete personal protective equipment). The President looks at the janitor and asks him what he was doing. The man looks up, identifies the President, and says, "Mr. President, I'm putting a man on the moon!" Whether true or not the point of the story is that the message had gotten through. The challenge President Kennedy issued

LEADERSHIP MANAGEMENT TOOLBOX

On May 25, 1961 before a joint session of Congress challenging the nation with the goal of sending an American safely to the Moon and back by the end of the decade had been transmitted and received throughout the organization. Communication is the most important yet least resourced, managed and directed function in today's work environment.

The next most important aspect is managing the development of our employees. Asking and answering the question to each individual, "what are you going to be doing five years from now?" and the corollary, "How are we going to get you there?" starts the process of The Becoming Principle. Providing the game plan and managing this process is not just important, it is absolutely essential to set the conditions for future success.

Process improvement is important at each level. Balanced Scorecard is the strategic Lean Six Sigma procedure senior management can use to focus, align, communicate and track performance.

Emotional Intelligence is what each of us uses to gage those qualities we look for in our employees as well as our boss. The best standard I have seen comes to us from the Bible, chapter 13, 1st Corinthians, verses 4-7. Replace the word "love" with either "my employee" or "my boss," it carries the same meaning: "My employee is patient, my employee is kind. My employee does not envy, does not boast, is not proud. My employee does not dishonor others, is not self-seeking, is not easily angered, keeps no record of wrongs. My employee does not delight in evil but rejoices with the truth. My employee always protects, always trusts, always hopes, always perseveres." The process we use should be managed and directed toward specific goals. In our culture we spend more time and effort selecting a jury than choosing a manager we will be depending upon to lead our work force to success.

SUMMARY CONCLUSION

Leader development is something we owe our employees. It also is something that will allow us to win the future.

I didn't create any of these tools, and have attempted to ensure the proprietary rights of those who did are protected. I have used them, however and know they function as advertised if properly applied.

Acknowledgments

There are many folks who deserve to be recognized and thanked for their contribution to this work and any measure of success it enjoys. My wife, Marti, is the single most important influence I have experienced; so much so that I no longer consider her to be separate or apart from me in any way. She and I are linked in so many ways it would be hard to try to determine where she ends and I begin.

Other than Martha, perhaps the most significant influence on this effort has been a man named Tom Green. The first time I talked with Tom Green I was sitting at my desk in Washington, DC where I was a staff officer in the US Army's Personnel Command. Tom called and congratulated me for being selected as one of his Battalion Commanders for his Aviation Brigade at Ft Bragg, North Carolina in the summer of '91. The first Desert Shield had just ended, and my wife and children were moving to Ft Bragg to work for Tom in the fall. Then later, after we both had retired from active duty and become managers in the private sector, Tom hired me to help him maintain a fleet of aircraft at Ft Rucker, Alabama, the US Army's Flight School. Tom is one of those Christians who actually live the Christian faith in day to day life. Tom taught me many things, but possibly the most precious gift being that you can be a Christian in today's world and become someone who influences others in the right way. It's not hard if you have a teacher like Tom. I remember him saying that he used what he learned in Sunday School more than what he learned in Business School to run his organizations. He would say that anybody can make decisions that cause more

ACKNOWLEDGMENTS

money to come in than goes out, and taking action to get more and more isn't really that difficult. The stuff he learned in Sunday School though is what we are called to do in every aspect of our lives and all walks of life. Tom knew that we should always choose the correct answer and to have faith that doing the right thing and acting on it will always be best. Tom influenced me in many other examples to have the "courage of my convictions" and to never be ashamed to express my faith and belief in God no matter what the audience or the reason. I realized after I stopped working with Tom how much his influence had impacted me. He showed me how to be normal and Christian at the same time whether it was politically correct to do so or not. I try to always remember the advice and guidance Tom gave me. I try to be the Tom Green in others just as Tom was to me and positively influence all those I come in contact with just as Tom does. He taught me how to properly manage leadership and how best to apply it.

Pat Thomas Resume

PROGRAM MANAGEMENT EXPERIENCE

- **Leadership** – Served with joint and international active duty military forces during all operational phases; planned, organized, directed and controlled units at all levels. Commanded at Company through Battalion levels providing mission, intent, vision, and ensured adjacent unit level coordination elements. Managed complex systems; possesses exceptional ability to communicate operational and strategic goals achieving mission accomplishment. Extensive experience developing personnel, enhancing internal processes and growth, product delivery, and performance sustainment. **(5 June 1974 – 31 July 2000).**
- **Aviation Logistics Sustainment Manager** – Twenty plus years aviation maintenance experience including Pilot, Aircraft Maintenance Officer, Test Pilot, and extensive maintenance, repair and overhaul sustainment activities; responsible for planning, directing, coordinating and managing support activities at each level. Responsible for manning, arming, fueling, fixing, transporting and protecting organizational assets from section through Corps levels. **(13 September 1976 – 31 July 2000).**
- **Director, Aviation Maintenance Program** – Senior Contract Maintenance officer for 35 aircraft and directly responsible for

PROGRAM MANAGEMENT EXPERIENCE

supervising a 350 plus, Unionized work force working a three shift operation, seven days a week. Program Manager for Organization's Balanced Scorecard: Strategic Planning and Performance. Published a 5 year strategic plan aligning the organization to the needs of multiple customers. Incorporated action plans to support strategic objectives; monitored and evaluated trends using the Balanced Scorecard methodology; streamlined, synchronized, and coordinated all external reporting requirements, taskings, and briefings. Enhanced communications with external customers as well as throughout the organization **(1 March 2004 – 1 November 2007).**

- **Director, Aviation Resource Management** – Managed maintenance services and Quality Control functions that ensured products and services delivered met internal and external requirements including legal compliance and customer expectation. Led the aviation maintenance effort required to sustain a 1250 member organization providing full spectrum maintenance services, quality control and aviation logistical support for 145 fixed and rotary wing aircraft operating out of seven countries (Central and South America and Mid-east) with fully compliant participation. Implemented winning successive contract option awards; achieved cost savings/avoidance through management concepts in development and management of contract Service and flight safety programs. **(1 November 2007 – 28 September 2010).**

- **Program Management** – Extensive experience, knowledge, skills and abilities, training and education in Project Management and the application of resources to achieve desired results. In depth experience and knowledge of aviation, aircraft maintenance, and production operations, scheduling, mission priorities and resource allocation, extensive knowledge of safety and security regulations, practices & procedures including HAZMAT environmental standards, regulations and requirements. Extensive knowledge of and experience in production control techniques, information technology, facilities management, work breakdown structure sequences, tooling, manpower and facilities requirements, mechanic, maintenance, and repair facility work processes and methodologies.

EDUCATION AND AWARDS

- Superior Award, Department of State, African Affairs; Defense Superior Service Medal; Legion of Merit
- Strategic Planning Degree, Foreign Relations and International Policy, United States Army War College.
- Masters Degree of Management, Webster University **(1990)**; Bachelor of Science, West Point, NY. **(1974)**
- Lean Sixth Sigma Green Belt Certified, University of Tennessee **(2006).**
- Lean Sixth Sigma Black Belt Certified, Villanova University **(2011)**.
- Project Management Professional, Certification 1228271

END NOTES: SOURCES OF INFORMATION

Covey, Steven. *The 7 Habits of Highly Effective People.* New York: Free Press, A Division of Simon and Schuster, 1989.

Moore's Law, *http://www.answers.com/topic/moore-s-law#ixzz1FGlykRnd*.

Massey, Morris. *The People Puzzle, Understanding Yourself And Others.* Virginia: Reston Publishing Company, Inc. / A Prentice-Hall Company, 1979.

Hannam, Susan and Bonni Yordi. *Engaging a Multi-Generational Workforce: Practical Advice for Government Managers.* Accessed February 9, 2011. *http://www.businessofgovernment.org/report/engaging-multi-generational-workforce-practical-advice-government-managers*.

Introduction to the Balanced Scorecard: Creating a Strategy Focused Organization from the Bottom Up, *http://www.balancedscorecards.com/article/intor/*.

Change Management ADKAR Model, *http://www.change-management.com/tutorial-adkar-overview.htm*.

Rawlinson, Graham E. "The Significance of Letter Position in Word Recognition." Nottingham UK: Unpublished PhD Thesis, Psychology Department, University of Nottingham, 1976. *http://www.mrccbu.cam.ac.uk/people/matt.davis/home.html/Cmabrigde/rawlinson.html*

INDEX

A

AAR (after-action review), 114-17
abilities, 63
ADKAR techniques, 35, 63, 66
assessment, 62, 85, 104
awareness, 63, 108

B

balanced scorecard
   benefits, 80-81
   concept, 13, 79, 83, 97, 103
   development, 84-85
   goal-setting and alignment, 85
   as a management tool, 79, 100, 103-4
becoming principle, 15
behavioral competencies, 56
boomers, 43

C

CCWF (contract civilian work force), 102
change, 68, 116
change management, 19, 97, 100
   concept, 61
   objectives, 63
   process, 35, 37, 120
communication planning, 21-23, 25, 27, 29, 32-34, 37
company core values, 81
corrective action planning
   concept, 119
   identifying problem areas, 121
   near-term actions, 123
   root-cause list, 124
   training initiatives, 124
Covey, Stephen R.
   7 Habits of Highly Effective People, The, 8
critique, 117
customer, hopes, wishes, and desires (HWD), 102
customer retention, 89
customers, 82
customer satisfaction, 102

D

delivery frequency, 34
delivery method, 32-33
"dirty bathroom," 33

E

e-mail, 9-11, 22-33, 43-44

INDEX

e-mail etiquette, 22-23, 26, 28-29
emotional intelligence, 15-16
employee commitment, 89

F

FACT process improvement activity, 62, 79
first-line supervisor focus, 37
Ford, Henry, 12
Franklin, Benjamin, 21
Frost, Robert, 10

G

goals, 36
Google, 77
group think, 97

H

hands-on approach, 18-19
Hannam, Susan, 42
  Engaging a Multi-Generational Workforce: Practical Advice for Government Managers, 42, 137
Harvard Business School, 13, 97
high performer, 49

I

IBM Center for the Business of Government, 42
individual change management, 62
initiative prioritization matrix, 94
initiatives, 82, 85, 93-95, 106, 108
intelligence quotient, 17

J

job effectiveness, 57

K

Kaplan, Robert, 13, 97
knowledge, 63

L

"laser beam" focus, 33, 39
leadership management, 12-13, 19
  goals, 48
  qualities, 49-51, 53
Lean Six Sigma Process Improvement, 19-20
Lean thinking, 12, 98

M

management, 96, 99
Massey, Morris, 40, 42
  People Puzzle, Understanding Yourself And Others, The, 40
Massey's theory of programming, 40
McDonald's, 98-99
medium, 32
millennials, 44
mission, developing strategies, 88
mission analysis, 85-88, 90
Moore, Gordon, 7, 20
Moore's law, 7, 20
Myers-Briggs Personality Assessment test, 18, 77

N

Norton, David, 13, 97

O

objectives, 85, 90, 106, 108
"open book" management, 81
operational excellence, 89, 91

organizational assessment analysis, 87-88
organizational change management, 62

P

P6T3SFI analysis, 74
parlor tricks, 76
People Puzzle, Understanding Yourself And Others, The (Massey), 40, 137
performance improvement plan, 54-55, 57-59
performance measures, 85, 92-94, 107
perspectives, 13, 82, 105
primary target audience, 33
process management, 99-101
process owner, 34
program manager, 83-84

R

reinforcement, 63

S

SEE (significant emotional event), 40
7 Habits of Highly Effective People, The (Covey), 8
SMART (specific, measurable, attainable, realistic, and timely), 90, 116
sponsorship, 67
staff call, 38, 71
standard operational procedure guide, 83-85
strategic initiative, 82, 103
strategic objective, 82, 90, 93
strategic results, 82
strategic themes, 82, 89-91, 93
strategy, 81, 83, 85, 105
strategy map, 82, 85, 90, 92, 107-8
success, 69
Sun Tzu, 11
supply chain, 88
SWOT chart, 105

T

target audience, 33, 35-36, 49
tasks
    implied, 85, 88, 106
    specified, 87-88, 106
task-to-objective conversion, 89-90
time management, 39
traditionalists, 42

V

vision, 35, 67-68, 81

W

"whole man" concept. *See* emotional intelligence
WIIFM (what's in it for me) concept, 33
working group management, 71

Y

Yordi, Bonni, 42
    Engaging a Multi-Generational Workforce: Practical Advice for Government Managers, 42, 137

www.ingramcontent.com/pod-product-compliance
Lightning Source LLC
Chambersburg PA
CBHW021956170526
45157CB00003B/1016